"Mary has crafted a book with a mix of fresh ideas along with tried and true examples of connecting with your grandchild. With six married children, fourteen grandchildren, nine great-grandchildren and two along the way, I have discovered that we never stop learning from them. I shall use *One-of-a-Kind Grandparent Connection* as a guide to bond. When closing the last page, one will feel the experience of enjoying a lovely conversation with the author."

—**Rita Goodgame** (Grandmother of 14 and Great-Grandmother of 11)

"Spending time with your grandchildren is one of the best investments you can make. But in this age of technology and long-distance grandparenting, many grandparents don't know how to connect with their grandchildren. Mary May Larmoyeux is passionate about helping grandparents find ways to engage with their grandchildren in unique and meaningful ways.

"Each chapter of *One-of-a-Kind Grandparent Connection* contains personal stories and practical ideas to help you invest in your grandchild's life. A great resource or gift for any grandparent."

—**Karen Jordan** (Grandmother of 8, Author of *Words That Change Everything*)

"What an outstanding book giving direction to so many people, young and old, on building relationships within a family. When putting into action many suggestions in this book, a family is also building memories that will be carried and cherished the rest of their lives.

"There isn't anything more wonderful than a strong family walking with the Lord and helping others to do the same."

—**Arlene Kirk** (Grandmother of 6 and
Great-Grandmother of 2)

"Mary has taken grandparenting to the next level of being intentional! She has networked with other grandparents and shares their experiences, as well as her own, in connecting with grandchildren in meaningful ways. Her personal stories of remembering the importance of her own grandparents helps bridge the significance of our legacy.

"*One-of-a-Kind Grandparent Connection* is formatted in a unique way that assists the reader to be intentional in practical application. At the end of each topical chapter, Mary not only lists sensible ideas for connecting with your grandchild, but also helps the reader follow through with the ideas they choose."

—**Joanie Stineman** (Grandmother of 7)

"Whether you are a new grandparent or a great-grandparent (as I am), our desire is to create lasting memories for our grandchildren. Mary May Larmoyeux has written a beautiful book about the various ways to connect with and inspire our grandchildren. I plan to use some of these suggestions to build an even stronger bond with my little ones."

—Delores Bull (Grandmother of 12 and
Great-Grandmother of 10)

One-of-a-Kind
Grandparent Connection

One-of-a-Kind Grandparent Connection

Building a Legacy with Your Grandchild

Mary May Larmoyeux

One-of-a-Kind Grandparent Connection
Building a Legacy with Your Grandchild

ISBN 978-0-9965743-2-7
Printed in the United States of America

Cover Illustration: Kinley Larmoyeux
Interior Text Design: Mary May Larmoyeux

Visit Mary May Larmoyeux at www.legacyconnection.org.

To my beloved grandchildren,
who someday will leave
a legacy of their own.

To grandparents who want to build
a strong relationship
with their grandchildren and pass down
a legacy of faith to future generations.

Contents

Foreword..13
Acknowledgments..15
Introduction..17

1. Begin Your Grandparenting Connection........21
2. Nearby Grandparenting....................................27
3. Long-Distance Grandparenting......................39
4. Your Prayers..51
5. Your Personal Stories......................................61
6. Your Faith Stories...71
7. Your Ancestors..83
8. Your Treasured Possessions 93
9. Your Family Photographs 101
10. Your Life Lesons 111
11. Your Unconditional Love..............................121
12. Your Family Recipes 129
13. Your Holiday and Birthday Traditions 139
14. Your Legacy...153

Appendix

• *My Grandparenting Connection*..............................163
• 10 Ways to Remember the Day
  a Grandchild Is Born.......................................171
• Christmas Do's and Don'ts for Mothers-
  and Daughters-in-Law 173

Foreword

Years ago, I had an epiphany while shopping with my grandson, Ethan. He was spending a few days with my husband and me, aka Poppa and Nonni. Anytime I picked him up to stay with us, I'd take him to the grocery store to pick out all the food he wanted, whatever he wanted, before going home.

On this particular visit, while walking the aisle with him, I had a flashback to how my grandmother, whom I named Mammie, did the same thing for me every summer when I visited her in Mississippi. Moments after my parents dropped me off, we'd get in the car and head for the store. And now here I was doing the same thing.

In fact, many of the things I do with my thirteen grandchildren today are a result of the seeds planted in my young soul by my grandparents.

My love of gardening and front porch swings came from my grandmother, Big Momma. My step-grandfather, Granddaddy Diehl—whom I loved equally, regardless of the moniker "step"—instilled in me the love of nature and hard work.

Granny Diehl gave me her love for cats and chickens. But her greatest gift was her example of holding her tongue. When someone spoke ill or gossiped about someone else, she'd just say, Wel-l-l?" and let it drop. Today I have cats and chickens for my grands to enjoy. And I'm reminded of her noncommittal, "Wel-l-l?" when I start to join a conversation I shouldn't.

I had another epiphany while reading Mary Larmoyeux's book, *One-of-a-Kind Grandparent*

Connection. My grandparents seeded within me their values just by their example, but how much more powerful and eternal would it be if we grandparented with purpose?

Every page in this book speaks toward intentionally connecting with our grandchildren. What we sow into them quite possibly will be sown into each generation long after we leave this earth. What a gift to the grandchildren we will never meet on this side of Heaven!

Reaching through the generations is the message you will find all through this book. The abundance of ideas and the gentle wisdom in every chapter whirled in my mind and motivated me. Of course, this is what Mary does in every aspect of her life. I've known her many years, and every suggestion is an extension of how she conducts her life. She is caring, faithful, and lives with purpose. How characteristic it is of her to share her gifts with us.

One-of-a-Kind Grandparent Connection is excellent for grandparents and for parents as well. It can help you make a positive impact in the lives of those you so dearly love. After all, when we interact with our grandchildren with intention—with purpose—the ripple effect will reach through future generations.

—Linda Apple, author of the children's book *Poppa's Very Special Sunflower* and other works, such as *Writing Life: Your Stories Matter* and *Inspire! Writing from Your Soul.*

14

Acknowledgments

Many thanks to the friends and family who encouraged me in the writing of *One-of-a-Kind Grandparent Connection*! Although it's impossible to express my appreciation to all who helped me craft this book, I want to thank the following people:

First and foremost, thanks to my husband, Jim, for his untiring love and encouragement. I would have given up writing this book if you had not inspired me to *keep on keeping on*.

Also, many thanks to my children and grandchildren. Without your stories, love, and support, I would not have written *One-of-a-Kind Grandparent Connection*.

Karen Jordan, thanks for your long-time friendship and tremendous help in birthing this book. I so appreciate your heart for grandparenting and your desire for grandparents to spiritually impact future generations.

Keely Boeving of WordServe Literary Agency, thank you for your enthusiasm for this book and for your belief that it should be published.

Many thanks to Perry County Writers whose insight into the organization of *One-of-a-Kind Grandparent Connection* was invaluable. I so appreciate your friendship and writing expertise.

How can I begin to thank those who took time to read the entire manuscript and give me their sincere comments? With warm gratitude I thank Delores Bull, Rita Goodgame, Karen Jordan, Arlene Kirk, Jim Larmoyeux, Margaret Sarkozi, and Joanie Stineman.

Linda Apple, I so appreciate you not only reading this manuscript, but also writing the foreword. I am honored that you did this and have learned a lot through your books, *Writing Life* and *Writing from Your Soul*. Your grandchildren are blessed to have such a loving, devoted grandmother as you.

And to my longtime friend Fran Taylor, thank you for your proofing and editing expertise. I am very grateful for your encouragement, wise suggestions, and eye for detail.

To the grandparents who left comments on my blog, Legacy Connection, or answered a survey question about grandparenting, thank you! Although I do not know all of your names, I want to express my appreciation to: Aileen, Allen, Andie, Ann, Arlene, Barb, Becky, Betty D, Betty M, Bob H., Brenna, Carla, Carol, Carolyn, Cassie, Cathy, Cheryl, Chris, Cindy, Cristal, Debbie, Deborah, Delores, Don, Doris, Elaine, Elisabeth, Ellen, Gabe, Glenda, Hallie, Helen, Janie, Janis, Johnnie, Karen, Kathy G, Kathy H, Kathy Y, Kenett, LaRue, Lewis, Linda, Lis, Lisa, Mary Ann M, Mary Anne G, Neal, Nick, Patty, Paulette, Perry, Rita, Sandra C, Sandra K, Shay, Sharon H, Sharon T, Shirley, Suzanne, Tamara, Teresa, Tommy, Toni, Tonya, Vicki, Vivienne, and Win.

Thanks so much for your transparency, ideas, stories, and desire to help other grandparents!

And most of all, I thank God who gave us the gift of family! As grandparents, may we connect to not only His heart, but also to the hearts of our grandchildren. May we make lasting memories and pass on family traditions and spiritual values to future generations.

Introduction

*My three-year-old granddaughter was pretending to take the
family dog to the dentist. "Darling, it's going to be okay," she
said to the dog. "Look me in the eyes. Calm yourself."*

—Mary May Larmoyeux

Nana...Pops...Mimi...Big Daddy... Cookie...
No matter your nickname, there is something
special about being a grandparent. After all, no one
in the world is exactly like your grandchild. They are
unique. One-of-a-kind.

And so are you.

Through the pages of *One-of-a-Kind Grandparent
Connection*, you will choose intentional ways to
connect with your grandchild. You are not striving
to be a *perfect* grandparent; there is no such thing. But
you are attempting to bond with nearby and long-
distance grandchildren, make lasting memories, and
pass on your values and family stories. In other
words, to build a legacy together.

But no matter where your grandchildren live, or
their particular situation, you can be a valued part of
their life. They may live nearby or far away, with
both mom and dad or with a single parent. You may
see a grandchild daily or not even once a year. And
your relationship with a grandson or granddaughter
may be wonderful in every way, or not very pretty.

Regardless of your circumstances, you can make
a positive difference in your grandchild's life and
impact generations to come.

Even simple things between grandparents and grandchildren can turn into lifetime memories. How many times have you watched in amazement as your grandchild shared their God-given talents with others? And do you remember when you laughed silently at something your grandchild said or did?

I was taking care of some grandkids one day, when a then three-year-old grandson didn't want to take a nap. After he had been in bed for maybe two or three minutes, he came out of his room, saying he had finished his nap.

"You have to sleep," I told him. "Your body will tell you when it's time to get up."

His response? "My body says it's time."

Well, back to his room he went…and two long hours later he woke up.

Yes, there can be so many smiles and shared memories between grandkids and grandparents: baseball games and piano recitals. Catching fireflies in the backyard. Gazing up at the sky and wondering together about the incredible creativity of God.

The connection you have with your grandchild can even be life-changing.

There's just something amazing about a grandparent interacting with their grandchild. Could it be that grandparents have seen how quickly life goes by? That they realize yesterday is gone and tomorrow is not promised?

Just imagine a generation you will never meet longing to personally say to you, "Thanks for caring. Thanks for taking the time. Thanks for preserving our family stories, and values, and faith."

Overview

One-of-a-Kind Grandparent Connection is filled with true stories, biblical applications, humorous illustrations, and creative ideas for grandparents.

Together, we'll journey through some of the questions many of us have, such as: "What will be my legacy? Why should I share the stories of my life? What can I do to preserve my family's history? How can I help future generations understand my values and faith?"

At the end of each chapter there are a few meaningful questions. Your answers to them will help you choose intentional ideas to invest in different areas of your irreplaceable grandchild's life.

At the back of the book, you will find an important section called *My Grandparenting Connection*. That is where you can jot down your favorite ideas as you think of connecting with your unique grandchild. You will refer to it often. So, you may want to put an index tab or bookmark at the beginning of that section.

Finally, there are some extra materials in the appendix: "10 Ways to Remember the Day a Grandchild Is Born" and "Christmas Do's and Don'ts for Mothers- and Daughters-in-Law."

A Question Only You Can Answer

As you think of your legacy, ask yourself, "Why do I want to connect with my grandchild?"

Maybe it's the perspective that comes with age. Perhaps it's the ability to reach across generations and share gifts or values that only you can communicate. Or, could it be that you now have an open, loving heart freed from some of the day-to-day stresses of raising your own children?

Whatever it is, your one-of-a-kind grandchild needs a connection with one-of-a-kind you. And so do generations yet to come.

Chapter 1

Begin Your Grandparenting Connection

We call our youngest four "middles and littles." Our youngest son crawled into bed with me one night and asked, "How old do you have to be to be a 'middle'?"

—Rebekah Hollaway

A few years ago, my then three-year-old grand-daughter pointed to a cross necklace I was wearing. "I like your 't,'" she said, not realizing it was actually a cross, a symbol of my Christian faith. I've never forgotten what she said in innocence that day. To her young eyes, my cross was simply a letter of the alphabet.

To be honest, at the time I thought her comment was kind of funny. She really thought I was wearing a "t." But now, years later, this memory reminds me that no one's faith is automatically accepted by the next generation. God works through parents and grandparents to pass down faith, the security of family, and lasting values.

You are important to not only your grandchildren, but also to generations yet to come. As Pastor Josh Mulvihill says, "God designed grandparents to be disciple-makers who treasure Christ, tell grandchildren the work of God, and teach grandchildren the truths of God's Word (Psalm 78:4-8)."[1]

When grandparents do that, they stand in the gap, connecting hearts and souls throughout generations. My daughter-in-law Tonya makes sure her kids know about her own grandmother. She said:

My grandmother was a woman who wasn't impressed by spotless kitchens. After all, who was she serving if her kitchen was clean but empty? She was a woman who didn't obsess about a little dirt on her floor. After all, clean floors don't tell the story of who's coming and going, or the work the family was able to do outside.

But you would be hard pressed to find dust on her Bible during her later years. That book was moved, used, read, and internalized. Mamaw left a profound impact on not only my life, but also on my perspective on life in general.

I remember walking into my dad's camper a few years ago, intrigued by the aging quilt across his bed. I recognized the handiwork—it was Mamaw's. My

[1]*Biblical Grandparenting* by Josh Mulvihill, © 2016 by Josh Mulvihill. Published by Legacy Coalition, a ministry of Awana, 25.

kids have been cuddled up with her makings for years. Although they have never met their great-grandma, they've heard many stories about her.

The quilt instantly reminded me of my heritage. You see, I come from a long line of hard-working women. However, this blanket looked different from others she had made. My dad told me that Mamaw sewed it from her husband's overalls after his clothes had seen their better days. The woman wasted nothing.

Now years later, the covering smelled like the woods. Dad spent days hunting and roughing it and then lay down to rest at night under my grandma's gift. Something in me didn't like seeing the quilt dirty, stained and torn.

I wanted to preserve it. Clean it and hang it somewhere so I could remember her. For a moment, I wanted to display it, so that it could be seen, to keep memories alive of the woman I miss so much. ...[2]

And it's not just how much our grandparents mean to us, but it's also how much our grandchildren teach us. Jean May said:

Grandparenting gives unending pleasure that would be impossible to cover in a few words.... It means so much to hear that little or not-so-little voice on the phone

---

[2] "Grandma's Quilt." Accessed on May 27, 2019. https://legacyconnection.org/grandmas-quilt. Used with permission.

calling to tell me of something special that happened at school that day or asking about something that happened in the "old days."

Grandparenting has taught me patience, understanding, and appreciation for my parents and grandparents. So much has become crystal clear to me now. I know my role in my grandchildren's lives is an important piece of their life's puzzle, and they're an important piece in mine.[3]

Because you are reading *One-of-a-Kind Grandparent Connection*, I think you long for a close relationship with each of your grandchildren. But maybe you wonder, "How do I begin to lay a foundation for that?"

First, look carefully at the chapter titles in this book. Each focuses on different aspects of grandparenting. Chapters 2 and 3 are filled with ideas for nearby and long-distance grandparents. Chapter 4 focuses on not only the importance of prayer, but also the many ways we can pray.

Chapters 5 and 6 deal with passing down your unique stories, while chapter 7 addresses your ancestors.

If you have treasured family possessions, chapter 8 will give you tips on preserving their history. And chapter 9 helps put an end to what I call "photograph madness." It gives specific ways you can organize those boxes of family photographs and countless electronic images of loved ones.

---

[3] Used with permission.

Do your grandchildren know why you are the person you are today…what you learned from your successes…from your failures? Chapter 10 will help you put down on paper some valuable lessons you learned in the ups and downs of your life.

Chapter 11 will remind you of the meaning of no-strings-attached unconditional love. After all, who among us has not disappointed a loved one or been disappointed ourselves?

Do you have some recipes that have been passed down in your family? Would you like to preserve them for future generations? Check out chapter 12.

Chapter 13 addresses holidays and birthday traditions. And then in chapter 14 we focus on leaving a legacy.

Finally, as mentioned in the introduction, you'll find an important section called *My Grandparenting Connection* (begins on page 163). You will refer to this often as you answer key questions.

PUTTING IT INTO ACTION

Well, are you ready to begin the journey of creating your unique grandparenting connection? You can start by answering these questions:

1. Why do you enjoy being a grandparent?

2. What have your grandchildren taught you?

3. What three chapters of this book interest you the most? Write these chapter titles below and also in *My Grandparenting Connection.*

4. Matthew 6:19-20 says: "Do not lay up for yourselves treasures on earth, where moth and rust destroy and where thieves break in and steal, but lay up for yourselves treasures in heaven, where neither moth nor rust destroys and where thieves do not break in and steal."

How can you apply this verse to your life?

5. What do you hope your grandchildren will remember about you? Answer below and also in *My Grandparenting Connection.*

Chapter 2

Nearby Grandparenting

Our two-year-old great-grandson, Caleb, said he wanted to be a fireman when he grew up, I asked. "Why a fireman, Caleb?"

He said, "Because they ride in the fire truck, and climb to upstairs windows where they save people from the fire." His little brow furrowed as he hesitated, then said. "But sometimes they take a hatchet and chop down the front door. FOR WHAT?"

—Rita Goodgame

More than fifteen years ago, Jim and I sat in a crowded waiting room of a nearby hospital, about to catch a glimpse of our first grandchild.

Our oldest son walked over to us with a huge grin and said, "It's a girl!" Immediately, joy swelled within me. And minutes later, Jim and I met our granddaughter face-to-face.

Until that moment, I had not understood why my grandparent friends often turned down invitations to lunch or to a party because they were "taking care of a grandchild." But now I understood.

As I was holding our granddaughter, I had a peek into our family's future…a living promise of a legacy…a hope for our family's tomorrow. And I was so grateful that Pops and I lived nearby.

If you are a nearby grandparent, you have many opportunities to connect not only heart-to-heart but also face-to-face with your grandchild. But just like long-distance grandparents, it will take effort to create a meaningful grandparenting connection.

Yes, you can be at birthday parties and school events, but grandparenting is much more than that. It's discovering the unique personality of your grandchild with various strengths and weaknesses. It's sharing your faith and values and letting your grandchild know your love is never-ending. That it does not depend on awards or grades, successes or failures. That's because your love is unconditional and grand.

Being a grandparent will cause you to do things you thought you never would. Like giving up a vacation to "grandsit" or learning how to text.

Years ago, did you imagine wanting to keep up with technology so you could be your grandchild's Facebook friend or Twitter follower? Yes, there is just something special about being a grandparent that can even cause us to get out of our comfort zone.

Poet Nora Hetrick describes grandparents as sprinkling stardust over the lives of their grandchildren.[4] And author Lois Wyse says,

---

[4]http://www.voicesnet.com/displayonepoem.aspx?poemid=114711, accessed February 12, 2019.

"Grandchildren are the dots that connect the lines from generation to generation."[5]

I picture those "dots" as great-grandparents… grandparents… parents… and their children joining hands with one another. Together they have vast life experiences stretching across multiple generations.

And with the passage of time, come many changes and challenges.

My parents went through the Great Depression and World War II. Jim and I remember black and white televisions and phones that had "party lines." And by the time Pops' and my youngest grandchild was born, iPhones and laptops were commonplace.

What about you? What changes have you seen in your life? Are you passing on your life experiences to your grandchildren?

How to Connect

Whether your grandchildren live nearby or far away, you will want to consider what connecting ideas will fit into your abilities and current place in life. There's a big difference between a forty-year-old first-time grandmother and an eighty-year-old great-grandmother.

But no matter your age, ask your nearby grandchildren what activity they would like to do with you. Some grandchildren might enjoy quiet

---

[5]https://www.goodreads.com/quotes/807103-grandchildren-are-the-dots-that-connect-the-lines-from-generation, accessed February 12, 2019.

one-on-one time. For them, you could go to the library together, look at old scrapbooks, or paint together.

However, if your grandchild thrives in a busy activity and you are physically able, consider things like horseback riding, hiking, or shopping together.

Of course, ask other grandparents for their connecting ideas. My friend Janice suggested spending one-on-one time with each grandchild. Doing this has helped her to get to know each child individually. As the number of our grandchildren increased, I understood the wisdom of Janice's suggestion.

For several years (before some grandkids moved out of state), all of our grandkids took turns having their "special weekend with Nana and Pops." We asked each child what they wanted to do on their visit and what they wanted to eat.

A five-year-old granddaughter was the first to have her special weekend. She wanted to learn how to draw a zebra or a giraffe. So, before her visit I arranged for a friend to give her an individual art lesson. Now a preteen, I think of that weekend long ago when I see the framed zebra hanging in her room.

We had *special* weekend requests to go to the park, play with "Mr. Potato Head," and learn how to sew. One older grandchild still enjoys reading on our porch and others like to swing in the hammock and play with the dog. And even though some of our grandkids are now teens, they occasionally play board games with Nana and Pops.

Pops takes each grandchild out for donuts on the Saturday morning of their special weekend. Now, please understand, we hardly ever eat donuts. But one time I had to chuckle when I overheard a grandchild tell a friend that her Nana and Pops always eat donuts for breakfast.

My friend Sharon Ball thought of her own grandfather as she watched an older man interact with a little girl in a restaurant. She recalls:

I miss my grandfather. He died over twenty years ago, but I think about him often. He especially came to mind a few weeks ago when my husband and I were having breakfast at a restaurant near our home.

We were seated across the aisle from a man who was sitting at a table with a little girl. At first, I thought the man was the little girl's father, but when she called him Papa, I figured out that he was, in fact, her grandfather. The thing that struck me about watching them was how sweet and gentle he was with this little girl, who was obviously his little princess. As she yammered on in her little-girl voice, he listened as if she were sharing the secrets of the universe.[6]

Sharon just expressed one of the reasons grandfathers and grandmothers are so special. Grandparents are quick to stop the hectic pace of life and exchange it for precious time with a grandchild.

Grandparents care. They love. They listen.

As a grandmother, I'm so aware that there are no guarantees of tomorrow, and I'm now realizing how

---

[6] Used with permission.

quickly the grandkids grow up. If you have nearby grandchildren, take time to regularly enjoy the simple things of life with them: walking in the rain, flying a kite, looking into the clouds together—marveling at the great God who created everything.

Here are some ideas for those of us fortunate enough to have nearby grandchildren. And if you have long-distance grandkids (as I also do), you may want to tuck away one or two of these ideas for their next visit.

ALL AGES

- **Take a grandchild to a local parade.**
- **Save dimes in a margarine container or jar.** When it's full, take your grandchild to the bank and deposit it into their savings account. Or ask your grandchild to give it to their church or a local charity.
- **Have a "cookie bake day."** Donna said her grandmother would bake more than 1,000 cookies in one day and freeze them in Kraft Velveeta® Cheese boxes. "We would be paid by the cookie box for doing tasks," she said. "When we visited, she would warm the cookies in a bun warmer...nothing better than warmed cookies and cold milk at Grandma's house."
- **Measure your grandchild's height** on the same door or wall. Mark their height, and jot down their name and the date.

- **Make homemade ice cream together** using an old-fashioned crank.
- **Shell peas** on the porch or deck.
- **Routinely give your grandchild the same special treat.** Sharon said, "My Pappaw bought me peppermint taffy."
- **Have family dinners** for nearby grandkids once a month. Arlene says, "We all sat around their big family dinner table enjoying the home-cooked meal, talking, laughing, and never distracted by outside objects…like cell phones."
- **Eat donuts together** and bring some home for the family.
- **Work in a garden together.**
- **Hang a bird feeder and watch the birds together.** Help older grandchildren identify the birds.
- **Point out the constellations** to your grandkids at night and talk to them about God's creation.
- **Work a simple jigsaw puzzle together.**

YOUNGER GRANDCHILDREN

- **Teach them how to make a potholder.** Plastic potholder looms are available at most hobby stores and on the internet.
- **Help them make an indoor fort.** The easiest way is to drape a sheet over a table.

- **Make up a story together when you are in the car.** You begin with "Once upon a time _____." Then the grandkids and you take turns adding to the story until it comes to a conclusion, or you arrive at your destination.

- **Teach them how to make paper dolls.** Or, buy some paper dolls and help your grandchild put them together.

- **Help the grandkids design their own cardboard dollhouse** and make cardboard furniture.

- **Play storybook "bingo."** For each grandchild, make a "bingo" card by drawing 16 squares on a piece of paper or cardboard (4 squares across and 4 squares down). Ask your grandchildren to choose 16 familiar words from a story you will read and to write those words in their card's squares.

  As you read the story, ask the kids to listen for the words they wrote on their cards. When they hear them, they can mark the appropriate squares. You may want to play straight-line bingo (cover four squares in a straight line in any direction), cover the card, etc.

- **Make a "bear hospital."** One of our granddaughters had a great time pretending that a stuffed bear was a patient in the hospital, and she was the doctor. All I had to do was supply bandages, a pillow, and a few blankets.

- **Go on a scavenger hunt.** You can make up your own clues for an indoor scavenger hunt or check out downloadable scavenger hunts on the internet.
- **Have an indoor picnic.** Just fill a basket with your lunch or dinner, and help the kids or grandkids pretend they are in the great outdoors. Spread out a tablecloth on the floor for your picnic. Wear hats and sunglasses and use paper fans. You may want the kids to help you plan the menu for your picnic and choose what you will bring to your indoor picnic. A game of checkers or indoor bingo could be fun picnic activities.

OLDER GRANDKIDS

- **Serve in a soup kitchen.**
- **Sort clothes together at a clothing closet for needy families.**
- **Prepare a meal with the grandkids for someone who is not well.** You may want to shop together for the ingredients.
- Teenage girls almost always enjoy **shopping!**
- Research your **family's genealogy** together.
- **Do a service project together** such as visiting an area nursing home or making a meal for a neighbor.
- **Talk to your grandkids about historical events** you have been part of, such as the

Vietnam War, Neil Armstrong walking on the moon, the September 11 attacks, etc. If you have pictures or news clippings of any of the events, share them with your grandchild.

- Encourage your older grandchild to ask you **questions about your life.** You may want to record this.

- Ask older grandchildren to teach you some form of **technology.** For example, how to use Facebook, how to text, etc.

- Look at **old family pictures** together. You may want to ask older grandchildren to help you sort through stacks of old photographs. If you need help organizing online images, you might want to ask a grandchild to help you with this, too.

- **Go to a local museum** together.

- Ask your grandchild to research upcoming **local events** and suggest one that you could do together.

- If you have **hobbies** such as fishing, sewing, restoring cars…enlist your grandchild's help.

- Go to a **movie or play** together. Afterwards enjoy a special meal or snack together and discuss whatever you saw.

- Tell your grandchild what it was like **when you were growing up** and talk together about the different pressures today.

PUTTING IT INTO ACTION

1. Think back to the first time you saw and held your first grandchild. What thoughts and feelings came to your mind and heart? Did this change your life in any way? If so, how?

2. Plan a "date" with each nearby grandchild, asking each of them what they would like to do. Allow ample time to listen and talk. Which grandchild will you take on a "date" first and what might you do?

3. Now look at the connecting ideas given in this chapter. Choose two or three you would like to begin. Write them below and also in *My Grandparenting Connection.*

Chapter 3

Long-Distance Grandparenting

Nothing better than getting a phone call from your young grandson saying, "Nana, I miss you. Can I come spend some time with you and just visit?" Be still my heart.

—Marty Paine (Nana)

One of the most important appointments of my week is a FaceTime call I have with my long-distance grandkids. Thanks to technology, Pops and I often enjoy a FaceTime visit with them, which allows us to see one another.

From the grandkids' side of the conversation, they often show Pops and me things that are important to them. And when we read children's books to the younger ones, we show them some pictures that are in the books.[7] The older grandkids show us their books and read the words to us.

---

[7] If you have a smartphone, there are many video call apps. If you do not have a smartphone, you could use an online video call program such as Skype. Hold the book so the grandkids can read along

Not too long ago, I was FaceTiming my two-year-old grandson and his four-year-old sister. She was eating a piece of apple when he asked, "Can I have some apple, too?" Thinking he would run into the kitchen and get a piece from his mom, I replied, "Sure you can."

But instead of heading to the kitchen, he stretched out his hands to the computer screen. Then he frowned when I did not slip him a sliver of apple. He was unaware that we were separated by cyberspace. I couldn't help but smile because he really thought I could give him a piece of fruit.

Although I was sorry I couldn't fulfill his request, there was a certain sense of satisfaction. Even though this grandson and I are not connected in location, we are connected in heart.

Somehow, in some way, with God's help, Pops and I are determined to connect with all of our grandkids. Connecting is just part of our hearts...part of God's heart. And I think connecting with your grandchild is part of your heart, too.

The Grandparent-Grandchild Connection

A few years ago, as I headed West to spend a couple of weeks helping with a brand-new grandson, I was reminded of the unique grandparent-grandchild connection. When a flight delay left me with unexpected time in the airport, I asked my fellow travelers about their grandparents. What made them special? How did they connect?

It was amazing how quickly conversations flowed! With a twinkle in their eyes, or a nod of the head, person after person was quickly transfixed by memories of a bygone age. An age when they felt the unconditional love of a grandparent. An age when the heart of their grandparent connected to theirs.

Devon's family lived with her grandmother off and on. One of her fondest memories is her grandmother scratching her back and then using her fingers to draw pictures, such as hearts and flowers. Now in her twenties, when Devon and her grandmother are reunited, guess what grandma still does? Yes, scratches her back and draws pictures.

A hotel shuttle driver said he was only six years old when his grandfather died. But before his grandfather left this world, he told his grandson story after story. One was about him fleeing to the United States from Austria when the German death squad was after him. The shuttle driver said his grandfather had a tremendous impact on his life, and today he is passing on the family stories that were told to him when he was just a young boy.

Shawn said that every summer his grandparents had all of his cousins visit them during the week of Vacation Bible School. The cousins attended it together, and they not only learned about the Lord, but also made memories he has never forgotten.

And Cathy shared a piece of truth: "You think your kids grow fast. Grandkids grow faster."

Ways You Can Connect with Your Nearby and Long-Distance Grandchild

No matter how passionate we may be about connecting with our grandchildren, our lifestyles and our limitations often get in the way of our desires. So, remember to make realistic choices that fit your abilities, interests, and lifestyle as well as those of your grandchildren. And ask the grandchildren what they would like to do with you.

Here are some nearby ideas[8] with adaptations for grandkids who live far away:

Nearby: Give your grandchild some new mittens or gloves in their favorite color. Buy a matching pair for yourself. When you do something outside with nearby grandkids on a cool day, remind them to wear their mittens, and you wear your matching pair.

Long Distance: If your grandkids live out of town, mail mittens to them with a picture of you wearing a matching pair. Then periodically call, email, or text your grandchild saying, "Today's our *blue* mitten day."

~

---

[8] *The Grandparent Connection: 365 Ways to Connect With Your Grandchild's Heart,* by Nancy Downing and Mary May Larmoyeux, © 2015.

Nearby: Make a favorite family recipe together. Tell the grandkids about the memories it brings to you and who gave you the recipe.

Long Distance: Mail the recipe along with needed ingredients. Depending on the age of your grandchildren, they can make the recipe themselves or ask Mom or Dad to help. You could video chat each other while making identical recipes. Or you could call your grandkids and tell them why the family recipe is special to you. I think you get the idea.

~

Nearby: Periodically take pictures with the grandkids and yourself. This is a great thing to do when you attend their school, church, and sporting events. For an extra touch, sometimes put one of these pictures in a magnetic frame for your grandkids' refrigerator.

Long Distance: When you visit the grandkids (or they visit you) take pictures with them. Later mail your grandchild a letter reminiscing your time together, and include some pictures. (Be sure to date and describe the pictures you send.)

~

Here are some more long-distance ideas from *The Grandparent Connection:*[9]

- Order pizza for your grandchildren and have it delivered to their home. By using the internet or calling long-distance, you can do this even if you do not live near one another. Ask your grandchildren to send you a picture of the "pizza party."
- Write a special note to your long-distance grandchild and ask their mom or dad to slip it into their lunchbox or backpack.
- Send a butterfly kit to your grandchild and purchase one for yourself. (You can purchase one on the internet.) Regularly compare one another's observations as you watch caterpillars change into butterflies.
- Go to the website of your grandchild's school and check out school events, sporting activities, etc. If their school has a newspaper, you may be able to read this online.
- Exchange Easter pictures via email, iPhone, or a photo-sharing website. Choose one of your grandchild's pictures and have mousepads made out of it—one for yourself and one for your grandchild.

---

[9]*The Grandparent Connection: 365 Ways to Connect With Your Grandchild's Heart,* by Nancy Downing and Mary May Larmoyeux, © 2015, 10-11, 18, 21, 22, 24, 29.

- Record some stories for your grandchild. Begin with an introduction such as:

    "_____

    (grandchild's name), *Nana and Pops* hope you enjoy this story about George Washington. He was the first president of the United States. We love you."

Your Own Traditions

Do you recall anything special that a grandparent routinely did with you? I remember my grandmother picking me up from school and always having a snack in the car. And if she made a "big cake" for the entire family, there would also be smaller, identical ones for the grandkids. She did these things over and over until they became a part of our unique connection.

One of my grandparenting traditions is to write each grandchild a letter for their birthday. Of course, there's no special way to do this. You could pen it by hand or use the computer. I've chosen to craft mine in digital format and mail a hard copy to the grandkids. In each letter I usually have:

- Color photographs of the child, taken during the past year, printed on the border of the letter.
- Reminders of what happened in the grandchild's life during that year–both joys and sorrows.

45

- A Bible verse that I will be praying for them during the year.
- A favorite memory I shared with the grandchild during the past year.

Pops and I both sign the letters, and we keep an identical copy that we file away. We will give each grandchild a set of their birthday letters when they are old enough to truly appreciate them.

Now, I have to confess, I often get behind on writing birthday notes. I have even mailed some for birthdays that have already passed. One year a grandson politely told me that I made a "typo" in his letter. I had said that I couldn't believe he's already ten years old when he had actually just turned eleven.

Oh, well, at least I tried. But I have to give myself grace and remember the letters will be special to the grandkids one day, even if they are late...even if they don't receive a birthday note every single year...and even if the letter has a "typo."

The Family Calendar

It was only this year that I realized how much our children and grandchildren enjoy the "annual family calendar." What began as a Christmas present idea more than a decade ago has become an annual tradition.

The calendar is made with the help of an online photo service. It has favorite pictures from the previous year, as well as reminders of family birthdays and anniversaries.

Last year was extremely difficult for our entire family as one of our children went through a painful divorce. At first, I thought it would be best to skip the family calendar.

But in the middle of January, long after Christmas had passed, one adult child quietly asked, "Are you going to do the family calendar?" He and his wife and their kids told me how much the calendar had meant to everyone because it had pictures of events that had happened during the previous twelve months. Unbeknownst to me, he said, "I've saved every calendar you've ever given us. They are like a family history."

Wow! I had never known that. And so, the family calendar came again this year...a little late but filled with so many wonderful memories that I had forgotten. Even the "broken family" is thrilled that the calendar continues.

As Pops and I look at it, we see happy faces at a family reunion, birthday celebrations, sporting events, school activities...It's still filled with reminders for birthdays, baptismal dates, and anniversaries. Bible verses are scattered throughout the calendar. What verse was used for February— the month of love? Psalm 32:10, "The LORD's unfailing love surrounds the one who trusts in him."

My Favorite Long-Distance Ideas

Back in 2011, I was given a beautiful blank journal with a beaded cover. It became the "Special Times at Nana and Pops' House" book. Whenever the grandkids spend the night at our house, we ask them to write a memory or draw a picture in it. That, too, has become a prized family tradition. And often when the grandkids come to the house, they will read through the journal and laugh at what they once said…or their cousins said.

We also have a special framed heart hanging in our kitchen. The heart is made of puzzle pieces, and each one was decorated by a member of our family. How was it made?

Well, I purchased a heart-shaped puzzle, and Pops sprayed it with white paint. Then we mailed some puzzle pieces to a long-distance son and his wife. We asked them, and each of their kids, to decorate a puzzle piece, sign it on the back, and then return the decorated pieces to us. (Where toddlers made their scribbles, their names were also printed.)

The family members who lived nearby decorated their puzzle pieces with Pops and me.

Today we have what to my eyes is a beautiful picture of family—a one-of-a-kind framed heart. It reminds me that no matter the shape of the "puzzle pieces of our lives" …no matter where any of us live…our love for one another will always bind us together.

Below our framed heart, we wrote our own message for our nearby and faraway family: "Whether we are near or far apart, each one of us is part of one heart!"

And this year Pops and I began a new long-distance tradition with old-fashioned roots. We are regularly writing letters to our faraway grandkids, using a different type of paper for each child, plus stickers for the little ones.

PUTTING IT INTO ACTION

1. Did any of your grandparents live far away from you? Do you have any special memories of spending time with them? If so, what made this time so memorable.

2. Listening is often the first step to getting to know a grandchild, or anyone. If grandchildren live far away, try to schedule a regular time to call or video chat with them. Jot below two or three questions that you would like to ask your grandchild:

3. No matter the age of our grandkids, we try to end our calls by blowing them a big kiss and telling them how much we love them. They often reply by blowing us a kiss, and we say something like, "It went straight to our hearts."

If you do not already have a unique way to end your conversations with your grandchild, and would like to do this, jot your ideas below.

4. Now look at the connecting ideas given in this chapter. Choose two or three you would like to begin. Write them below and also in *My Grandparenting Connection.*

Chapter 4

Your Prayers

Our prayers may be awkward. Our attempts may be feeble.
But since the power of prayer is in the one who hears it and
not in the one who says it, our prayers do make a difference.

—Max Lucado

Evangelist Sammy Tippit never met his grandmother. For years she was just a name in his family tree. But that changed when he was researching his family roots and found a description of his grandmother written by an aunt.

His aunt said Sammy's grandmother "could talk to her Redeemer better in her garden," and described her as "a meek, God-loving person. She lived close to God, loved her church, husband, and children. She totally trusted God for all her needs."

"… I had no idea that my grandmother was a mighty woman of prayer,"[10] says Sammy.

You see, he had grown up thinking he had no Christian heritage. His parents seldom attended

---

[10]*Praying for Your Family* by Sammy Tippit, 17-19, © 2006 by Sammy Tippit. Published by Sammy Tippit Ministries.

church. When he placed his faith in Christ, his mother did not understand.

"After learning about my grandmother," Sammy said, "I realized she died not having seen the answer to her prayers for my dad. Yet twenty-three years after her death, God reached down and saved her grandson—a grandson she never met. Two years after that, her grandson's life would be used of God to bring her son to Christ."

Grandparents, our prayers matter!

Focus on Who God Is

Like Sammy's grandmother, David was a man after God's own heart (1 Samuel 13:14, Acts 13:22). What did he do with his worries? Let's go to Scripture and find out.

In 1 Samuel 21-23 we read of King Saul pursuing David, wanting to kill him. Saul's jealousy for David had turned into murderous rage. David wrote Psalm 54 during one of Saul's mad pursuits:

> O God, save me by your name,
> and vindicate me by your might.
> O God, hear my prayer;
> give ear to the words of my mouth.
>
> For strangers have risen against me;
> ruthless men seek my life;
> they do not set God before themselves. *Selah*

Behold, God is my helper;
the Lord is the upholder of my life.
He will return the evil to my enemies;
in your faithfulness put an end to them.

With a freewill offering I will sacrifice to you;
I will give thanks to your name, O LORD,
for it is good.
For he has delivered me from every trouble,
and my eye has looked in triumph on my enemies.

"When David was under stress," says the Precept Upon Precept® study of 1 Samuel,[11] "basically he laid the situation before God, then focused on who God is, what God is able to do, and his status before God. Then he rested in those truths, either by requesting His help, affirming His redemption power, or praising and thanking Him for being God."

We can do the same. By faith—not by feeling.

Are you going through a difficult situation with a grandchild? Perhaps you're feeling like one of my friends who said, "It's hard to hang on [to God]. Sometimes I want to let go."

Or another who said, "I feel like I am dancing and I can't dance any faster."

Tell God about your problem, and then focus on who God is and what He can do. Remember that you are a child of God, and that He loves you. He wants the best for you and your grandchildren.

---

[11] *1 Samuel: God's Search for a Man After His Own Heart*, 2nd ed. (Chattanooga, Tennessee: Precepts Ministries International © 2013), 72.

As I mentioned in chapter 3, my husband and I are going through a hard season now—heartbroken because one of our children has divorced. Some of our grandchildren's lives seem to be ripping apart. And time and time again, I have turned to Scripture looking for answers.

A portion of one of my journal entries, based on Psalm 23, says:

> *Lord, be their shepherd. Give them hope and not fear. May they all look to You and find Your never-ending peace. A peace that makes no earthly sense in the midst of so much heartache.*
>
> *... May they discover Your "still waters" in the midst of turbulence. And the still waters are You.*
>
> *... Even in this deep valley of their lives help them to know that You are with them. Comfort them—only You can do this.*
>
> *Almighty God. work even this for Your good purposes. We trust You.*

It's often easier to trust our own abilities than God's—to try to help a grandchild instead of waiting on Him in prayer. Peter Marshall said, "Teach us, O Lord, the disciplines of patience, for to wait is often harder than to work."[12]

---

[12] BrainyQuote.com, BrainyMedia Inc, accessed August 15, 2019. https://www.brainyquote.com/quotes/peter_marshall_385781.

Waiting on God is not easy for me. It relies not only on believing God is who He says He is, but also trusting He can do what He says He can do in His time.

One of the most important things we can do for our grandkids is to pray and wait on God for His answer. Psalm 5:3(NIV) says, "In the morning, O LORD, you hear my voice; in the morning I lay my requests before you and wait expectantly."

Holocaust survivor Corrie ten Boom said, "Is prayer your steering wheel or your spare tire?" I want prayer to be the steering wheel of my relationship with my grandkids. I want them to know that I am praying for them in the good times and bad. I want them to know that sometimes I struggle to trust God, but choose to do so anyway. After all, He will meet all of their needs when I don't know how.

What if you aren't sure exactly *how* to pray for your grandkids? As a prayer guide, I use the book *While They Are Sleeping: 12 Character Traits for Moms to Pray.*[13] It gives specific verses to pray for character traits such as kindness, humility, teachability, forgiveness, obedience, discernment, purity, responsibility, courage, servanthood, contentment, and endurance.

I have a copy of this book for each grandchild and jot down the dates I pray for each of them. Funny thing…often I find myself not only praying

---

[13]*While They Were Sleeping: 12 Character Traits for Moms to Pray*, by Anne Arkins and Gary Harrell, © 2004. Published by FamilyLife. Little Rock, AR.

the verses in this book for my grandkids, but also for Pops (Jim) and myself and our children.

Our grandkids know that I pray through these books for them. I actually asked each of them to write something at the beginning of each book. It touched my heart when a then nine-year-old granddaughter wrote inside the cover of her copy of *While They Are Sleeping*, "This is very special to me."

Using this book helps me set aside dedicated time to pray for each of my grandkids—but there are many other ways to do this. The key is to find what works for you, and to make it a regular part of your daily routine. By laying the foundation of daily prayer for your grandkids, you'll usually turn to God first when things start to get difficult or you find yourself in a time of real anxiety.

Here are some more ideas about prayer:

- Ask your grandkids how you can pray for them and remind them that God really does hear and answer our prayers.
- Keep a list of your grandchild's prayer requests along with answered prayers.
- Pray for your grandchild's requests. Then follow-up by asking your grandchild about them. If they are frustrated that a particular request hasn't been answered, you might tell them about a similar experience in your own life when you had to wait on God's timing.
- Share some of your own prayer requests with your grandchild. And ask your grandchildren to pray for you.

- Share answered prayers: One grandmother told me that her granddaughter had been praying for her to get $1,000. When this grandmother unexpectedly received a check for a dollar in the mail, she called her grandchild to let her know that she had received some unexpected money. The granddaughter was thrilled!

- Purchase a Bible for a particular grandchild and use it during a calendar year to pray through for him. You may want to begin doing this on a grandchild's birthday and give it to him the following year.

- Jot down dates when you pray certain verses, and sometimes include a little prayer on the page for your grandchild.

As the Lord leads you, pray throughout the day for your grandchild. Sometimes send her a text, email, or letter letting her know you were doing this. My friend Elaine writes a prayer for each of her grandchildren. And grandmother Kathy (GiGi) says it's important to pray for every aspect of our grandchildren's lives, including their safety and protection.

Shaping Your Worries Into Prayers

God has given each of us unique personalities with different strengths and weaknesses. As Karen

Jordan wrote in *Words That Change Everything*,[14] "We must always be aware of our weaknesses, vulnerability, and complete dependence on God."

Karen says to consider the following strategies[15] whenever we begin to convert worries into prayers:

1. Examine your emotions. Are you worried? Depressed? Afraid? Sad? Confused? Stressed? Fill in the blanks to examine why you feel that way.

I'm _____

because_____.

Example: I'm worried because my grandchild is moving away, and I'm not going to be able to see him very often.

2. Write some details about whatever is troubling you right now concerning your grandchild.

Example: I'm worried because my grandchild just moved out of our home after living with us for six years. And I'm also sad that he will be living across town, and I probably won't be able to see him every day.

3. What promises did you find in God's Word that could help you pray for your grandchild?

Example: Philippians 4:5-6 (NIV) promises, "…The Lord is near. Do not be anxious about anything, but in every

---

[14]*Words That Change Everything* by Karen Jordan. © 2016 by Karen Jordan, Leafwood Publishers, 125.
[15] Used with permission.

situation, by prayer and petition, with thanksgiving, present your requests to God."

4. Write a specific prayer for your grandchild. Here's an example:

Lord, thank you for reminding me that you are always near. Help me not to be anxious about my grandson moving away. And teach me to turn all my worries into prayers. Amen.

When you find yourself worried about your grandchild, remember these words from the Bible paraphrase *The Message*: "Don't panic. I'm with you. There's no need to fear for I'm your God. I'll give you strength. I'll help you. I'll hold you steady, keep a firm grip on you" (Isaiah 41:10).

How Can We Pray for You?

As grandparents, isn't it wonderful to know that we can trust God with our grandchildren...that He wants to hold them steady! That's especially evident to me when we talk with our grandsons and granddaughters.

When Jim and I call our long-distance grandkids, we often ask them three questions: "How are you helping others?" "What are you learning about God?" and "How can we pray for you?"

Even though we live a long way from these grandkids, God has a grip on them! One day, when we asked a four-year-old granddaughter what she is learning about God, she said, "I'm learning not to forget about God, even when I'm mad at Him."

Her six-year-old sister once said, "God never stops loving you even when you mess up."

And when her family was visiting churches, one little granddaughter said, "We didn't get to church in time to hear the message about God. But I liked the snacks! That was my favorite church!"

PUTTING IT INTO ACTION

1. How have you seen God answer your prayers?

2. What would you like God to do in the life of your grandchild?

3. What promises do you find in God's Word that could help you pray for your grandchild's specific needs?

4. What is one prayer idea from this chapter that you would like to begin? Write your answer below and also in *My Grandparenting Connection.*

Chapter 5

Your Personal Stories

A granddaughter had visited a nursing home and was telling me about the people with the "broken bottoms." I had no idea what she was talking about until her mother explained: She had thought people were in wheelchairs because their "bottoms broke."

—Mary May Larmoyeux

How would you feel if you found your father's love letters to your mother in a dust-covered box? What would you think if an internet search gave a surprising answer to how your ancestors came to America?

I don't know exactly how my family got to this country. But about twenty years ago I was given a copy of my grandfather's memoirs. It was a wonderful surprise!

Grandpa began by saying he didn't know if anyone would even care about his words. That his idea of a memoir came in 1929 when the Great Depression began. "There being plenty of cares, but little business to distract my attention," he said.

As a child, I never asked my grandparents about their childhoods, the Great Depression, or World Wars. And over the years I've wondered, "Why not?"

Now in my sixties, I think the answer is the same reason our grandkids don't ask us about the protests of the sixties, the Vietnam War, or where we were during the 9/11 attacks back in 2001. They don't realize that we have lived through history, and often, neither do we.

I'm so glad Grandpa wrote about his childhood and many of his life experiences! But, looking back now, I would be even more grateful if we had talked about the things that mattered to him.

Grandparents and grandkids usually talk about the everyday events of life—the next soccer practice, a church event or school play. I am guilty of this myself, not really thinking that I may not have tomorrow.

Grandpa's tomorrow came when he was in his eighties, and he was buried in a cemetery where many of my relatives are laid to rest. Years ago, I was curious about who was also buried there, so Jim and I made a visit to "see my grandfather and the family."

Our day began with one of the burial ground custodians opening a huge, dusty book and pointing to the names of some of my ancestors. Then the man marked the plots of deceased family members on a cemetery map. He gave it to Jim and me, and as we left his office he said with a merry laugh, "Have a good family reunion!"

I smiled at what seemed like a humorous remark, but by the end of that day I had changed. I felt like I had somehow touched part of my family history that had been foreign to me.

I stood before the graves of beloved grandparents, an aunt I'm named after, and relatives who died too soon. I touched the grave markers of a great-grandmother and great aunt I never knew. Oh, how I wished those dry bones could have danced that day, that they could have spoken, that there truly could have been a real family reunion.

How I wished that relatives I had never met could have told me about their lives and families, hopes and dreams, successes and failures.

If you've stood before the graves of beloved grandparents, you may have had similar feelings. What stories of their life do you wish your ancestors shared with you?

Agi Geva

Yes, it's important for us to share about our lives while we can.

Years ago, Jim and I heard Holocaust survivor Agi Geva[16] tell about her experiences during World War II. We watched her roll up her sleeve, revealing her concentration camp identification number.

Agi did not want the numbers removed. Why? Because it was a reminder to herself and others to "Never forget!"

---

[16]"Agi (Laszlo) Geva, " https://www.ushmm.org/remember/office-of-survivor-affairs/survivor-volunteer/agi-laszlo-geva.

Until I heard Agi speak, I had never really thought much about the history I've experienced. To me, it was so... "usual." But as I heard her message, I was reminded of the responsibility and privilege of sharing the events of my life with my children and grandchildren.

What pieces of history have you lived through in your lifetime? What life lessons do you want your children and grandchildren to remember? Where were you on September 11, 2001, when New York City's Twin Towers fell down? How did you feel?

I was at home, and my husband called and said to turn on the TV...that something terrible had happened. Minutes later I was watching one of the massive towers of the World Trade Center crash down. My initial thought was, *What kind of horrible aviation accident caused this?*

And then I joined untold numbers of people around the world huddled by TVs. Together we watched another plane hit the second tower. The crumbling structure was no accident. And the lives snuffed out in seeming moments were no chance event. What began as an ordinary day quickly turned into one the world would never forget. We were not just witnessing history; we were part of it.

How to Begin Writing Your Stories

If you have school-aged grandchildren who live nearby, you have likely looked at their art work and papers displayed on class bulletin boards. Well, not long ago I was reading first graders' thoughts on what it would be like to be 100 years old.

Many of the kids wrote about wrinkles, and canes, and watching as much TV as they wanted to. But one little boy's paper caught my eye. Here are his words: "First, I would start writing a journal. Then, I would wear pjs and glasses. Last, I would say get [off] my lawn. I would write about my adventures."

What life adventures do you want to write about?

What everyday moments do you want to remember?

Here's an example of an everyday moment that Karen Jordan had with her grandson Ben. They were watching a movie together about four young children who had run away from home. In the movie, the children's parents had died, and they did not want to live with a grandfather they had never met.

Why? Because they thought their grandfather didn't love them as he had never visited them while their parents were alive.

At the end of the movie, when the children finally met their grandfather, Ben turned to Karen and said, "Nonnie, I know you love me. You come to see me all the time, right?"

Holding back tears, Karen kissed her grandson on the forehead. "I sure do, Ben!" she said. "I love you, and I like you."

Ben laughed at his grandmother's response because he had told Karen numerous times, "I love you, and I like you, Nonnie."

Karen's everyday moment with Ben wasn't lost because she wrote it down. And I could have easily lost what now is a favorite memory of mine.

Years ago, when I was at a writers' meeting, the speaker set a timer and said to write about the rain. There had been a recent thunderstorm when a grandchild was visiting, so I wrote the following about it:[17]

God Himself entertained my almost two-year-old granddaughter as she sat with her chubby legs propped in the windowsill, content to rest on a short six-inch stool.

She squealed when the patter of raindrops became a steady downpour. She clapped her hands after the heavens bellowed into a thunderous chorus.

She stood up and pressed her soft face against the cool pane of glass while flashes of lightning danced through the afternoon sky.

I had survived one more dreary afternoon of yet another day of rain. But my two-year-old granddaughter had witnessed a stirring performance of nature—one deserving an encore by a child enthralled by life.

A Timeline of Your Life

What are some of your favorite memories of everyday moments with your grandchildren? What life adventure do you want to tell ancestors you will never see?

Remember these words of American educator John W. Gardner, "History never looks like history when you are living through it."

---

[17]"Through the Eyes of a Child," by Mary May Larmoyeux. © 2002.

Karen Jordan agrees: She is not only my friend and an author, but also a writing instructor. When someone asks her how to begin a personal story, she suggests: [18]

- Draw a timeline of your life, dividing it into five- or ten-year segments.
- As you draw your timeline, list five to ten memories.
- Jot down on the timeline some dates and events that you want to remember. Ones that relate to significant people, places, events, or crises in your life. Include times of significant growth, maturity, and change.
- Decide what kind of paper you want to use: lined, unlined, or construction paper. And will you use pencil, crayons, a pen, or an electronic device?
- Pick one memory from your timeline (of a person, place, or event) as a starting place.
- Brainstorm your memory. Include sensory descriptions (sight, sound, touch, etc.). You can do this by writing ideas, sentences …even drawing a picture—perhaps of your childhood home.

How many stories should you write? That's up to you. Just do your best to capture your adventures and everyday memories for future generations.

---

[18]Karen Jordan is the author of *Words That Change Everything* and *Rest Notes*. You can visit her at www.karenjordan.net. Used with permission.

Your stories could be written as long books or short poems. They may be jotted down on the backs of photographs or written in calligraphy and put in fancy frames. You may even want to write your own autobiography, or ask a loved one to do this.

After my dad passed away, I asked my mother to write about her life. She jotted her memories in a yellow spiral notebook. I have to laugh now as I think of my sweet mom keeping that notebook under a couch cushion. It was our "secret."

When I visited Mom, she'd often pull out the notebook and proudly tell me that she had written some more. For Christmas one year I typed what Mom wrote, added some pictures, and gave a copy of "Mom's book" to family members.

What she wrote was not long—perhaps 2500 words (about 10 pages). Yet, there are no words to describe how glad I am that she did this. And how I wish I had asked my dad to do the same!

What happened to the yellow spiral notebook? When Mom was alive, I did not realize its worth. But thankfully I did not throw it away. Much older now, when I see Mom's handwriting on the lined pages, I realize the value—priceless!

PUTTING IT INTO ACTION

As you brainstorm about your story, ask yourself, "Who will read it—your children, grandchildren… generations you will never see?" Now, it's time to write.

1. Begin by looking at your timeline, memories, and other notes or drawings. Set a timer for 10 minutes and see how much you can write in that short length of time.

2. Don't get bogged down in writing something perfectly. Ignore grammar, spelling, punctuation, neatness, and style—you can revise it later.

3. Keep writing—even if you get stuck or veer off topic.

4. When the timer goes off, you have the beginning draft of your first story. Either stop now and make an "appointment" to finish the story (step 5 below), or finish your initial thoughts.

5. Make a one-hour appointment with yourself this week to continue working on your first story. Set a reminder on your phone or alarm clock. During this appointment, ask yourself the following questions:

- Do I need to add to this story? If so, what?

- Should I remove anything from this story?

- Are there pictures that I want to scan into digital format for this story? Are there family members who I want to interview?

6. Write the working title of your first story below and also in *My Grandparenting Connection.* Also jot down when you want to finish this story and where you will keep it. (You may want to not only keep an electronic copy of your story, but also put a paper copy in a 3-ring binder.)

7. Look at the list of memories that came to your mind as you drew your timeline. Now choose one for your second story. Briefly describe this memory below and also in *My Grandparenting Connection.*

Chapter 6

Your Faith Stories

My grandson said, "Can I play in heaven? Will there be food there I like?"

Then his sister piped in, "Do I have to sleep when I get in heaven? And I want to bring my teddy bear. What if there are NO teddy bears in heaven?"

—Mary May Larmoyeux

Have you told your grandchildren, in written or spoken word, why you believe what you believe? Do they know when God drew you to Himself?

Do they know about the faith of your parents? Whether you are in close contact with your grandchild or rarely see them, do you believe that God can still use you to make a spiritual impact on their life and future generations?

Are you aware of the teachable moments you have with your grandchildren? And what spiritual lessons can they learn from your life, their parent's life, or even from things they have said or done?

Marilyn's Story

Years ago, Marilyn told me about something that happened to her now adult son, Adam, when he was about four years old. At the time, she was a teacher at a small Christian school, and he was in preschool there.

"Adam was one of those children," she said, "who was blessed with a high IQ, but had trouble listening and following rules in a structured environment."

Well, the playground at Adam's school was covered in tiny pebbles, and Adam stuffed his pockets with them every time he was on it. His preschool teacher had asked him not to do this. But no matter what she said to him, after recess, his teacher always found little pebbles in the toilet, the play area, and even on Adam's sleeping mat.

When Marilyn learned about Adam's obsession with rocks, they had a little chat. She told him not to put even a single pebble into his pocket during school. "We had him repeat the rule," she said, "and he clearly understood."

The day after that conversation, Adam's teacher checked his pockets as they were leaving the playground, and they were empty! Naturally, when Marilyn heard the good news she was overjoyed. And when she saw Adam, she congratulated him, thinking the problem was solved.

At bath time, Marilyn heaped praise on Adam for his empty pocket. "But when I started removing his Ninja Turtle Underoos," she said. "Suddenly dozens of pebbles came spilling out. I was taken aback that he had blatantly disobeyed us that way."

Adam was not dismayed. "Mommy," he said, "You said no rocks in my pockets. You didn't say I couldn't put them in my underpants!"

When Adam turned around, Marilyn saw his backside covered with little indentations from the pebbles. He had sat on them all day. The pebbles had meant more to him than being comfortable.

"We know God sees and hears everything," Marilyn said, "and yet we embrace a spiritual denial as though we're getting away with it. Just like my little son's backside, we are left with sore and scarred lives."[19]

Your Spiritual Stories

What spiritual story could you tell your grandchild? The ideas are endless, but here are a few:

- Something your grandchild did that had a spiritual meaning
- Your family's faith tradition when their parent was growing up with you
- Your parents'/grandparents' faith

---

[19]"He Had Rocks in His Pocket," April 25, 2014. https://storywritingstudio.wordpress.com/2014/04/25/he-had-rocks-in-his-pocket. Accessed on May 27, 2019. Used with permission.

- When you made faith your own
- What a typical Sunday was like for you growing up
- Your thoughts about God and life on the day they were born
- Why a particular verse in the Bible has great meaning for you
- What Jesus means to you
- Your greatest struggle believing God when you were growing up
- A time when you were disappointed with God
- A time when you were overwhelmed with praise for God.
- What you think about God when you see a sunset
- How you learned to bring your cares to God
- A way God answered a difficult prayer
- Your spiritual hopes for your grandchild
- How the faith of your teenage friends made a positive or negative difference in your life
- When you, your grandchild's parent, or your grandchild was baptized
- A spiritual word written in a Bible

Jay Grelen, who wrote the *Sweet Tea* column for the *Arkansas Democrat-Gazette*, once told his readers about Little Grandmama. He had found her Bible, and it had only one line of handwriting: "Tribulation worketh patience. Romans 5:3."

74

Jay wondered what Little Grandmama was thinking as she penned those words. "Her inscription is a word from beyond," he said, "A pebble she dropped exactly at the spot on my trail where I needed guidance."[20]

How to Tell Your Spiritual Stories

Deuteronomy 4:9 (NLT) says: *"Watch out! Be careful never to forget what you yourself have seen. Do not let these memories escape from your mind as long as you live! And be sure to pass them on to your children and grandchildren."*

God has worked through unique trials and blessings in your life to make you, "you." But how can one-of-a-kind-you and one-of-a-kind-me communicate our spiritual stories to our grandchild? Here are some possible ways:

- Write your story in a journal.
- Sing it in a song and record it.
- Jot short spiritual lessons in a Bible.
- Naturally share spiritual applications in everyday conversation with your grandchild.
- Write a poem.
- Call an older grandchild and tell them about a spiritual lesson you learned (then write the lesson down).

---

[20]"Little Grandmama," https://grandconnection.blogspot.com/search?q=Little+Grandmama. Accessed on April 21, 2019. Used with permission.

- Leave your written spiritual story in a special box. Write a letter about what God has taught you. Either mail it now or give it to a grandchild when they reach a certain age.
- Videotape your story.
- Put your stories in a bound book.
- Use a tape recorder. (Yes, they still make them.)
- Record your story using a hand-held digital recorder. Use one that allows you to transfer the recording to your computer. Consider burning a CD with your story and giving it to your grandchild.
- Paint a picture of a spiritual story in your life, and on the back of it tell why it has meaning to you.
- Take a picture of something that represents a spiritual lesson you have learned. Then write on the back of it why it has this spiritual meaning to you. Be sure to date and sign the back of the picture.

You can tell your faith stories in many ways. The important thing is to save them for future generations.

Years ago, one of our grandchildren did something that touched my heart, so I jotted the story down. She had spent days coloring Valentine cards when her dad discovered a small envelope on the front porch. In the obvious handwriting of a child, it was addressed to G O D.

"Sweetheart," our son asked as he pointed to the printing, "What's this?"

"Oh," she replied as she looked up at her father with her big blue eyes, "I'm sending a Valentine's card to God. I left it on the porch so the wind would blow it up to heaven."

Footprints of Faith

In *Legacy of Prayer*, Jennifer Kennedy Dean tells a story about a woman named Wendy who was looking through a box of faded family photographs. Dean writes:

Wendy came across a brittle piece of lined paper. The writing on it was faint, but she could make out the words of a handwritten prayer penned by her father's grandmother. "This day, July 10, 1912, I hereby sign and give my son Robert over to the Lord, for the Lord to redeem his soul from sin and make him an earnest Christian." Wendy had found what she now calls "a footprint of faith in a family that had seemed singularly godless."[21]

How have you seen the faithfulness of God in your family?

My childhood home was a strong, loving family of faith. Yet, I didn't understand what it meant to have a personal relationship with Jesus Christ. That changed when I went to college. Going from a high school class of less than 100, to a university campus

---

[21]*Legacy of Prayer: A Spiritual Trust Fund for the Generations*, by Jennifer Kennedy Dean, © 2010 Jennifer Kennedy Dean. Cross House Publishing, 25.

with more than 20,000 students, was overwhelming. Sometimes I felt lost. And whenever I thought about eternity, there was a sense in my soul that I could never do enough or be enough to enter God's presence.

That's when a friend said I didn't have to do more or be a better person to be right with God. She explained the meaning of Romans 3:23-24: "For all have sinned and fall short of the glory of God, and are justified by his grace as a gift, through the redemption that is in Christ Jesus." I accepted that grace, and my life changed forever. I discovered the lasting peace I had been searching for.

Then several years later, my husband, Jim, discovered that same peace. This happened when our oldest child was born two months early and was not expected to live. Jim asked God to not only make his own relationship with Him right, but also to save our struggling son. In God's mercy and grace, He answered both prayers.

I have one final example for you. It's the beginning of a poem called "Grandma's Stories" that my daughter-in-law, Tonya, wrote when she was a teenager:

> *"So I listen to the stories,*
> *that Grandma told so well,*
> *so I can say to my kids,*
> *'Those were the stories*
> *my Grandma used to tell.'"*[22]

---

[22] Used with permission.

Today Tonya is telling Grandma's faith stories to my grandchildren. And they will tell them to their children. What a legacy Grandma has...what a "footprint of faith"!

Giving Hope to Future Generations

As a grandparent, does it give you chills to think one of your stories could be used by God to encourage a great-great-great-great grandchild? Perhaps in generations to come, their fingers will trace over your handwritten words jotted down on the back of a faded picture or in a worn Bible. Maybe your grandchildren will silently thank you for giving them a legacy of hope...for reminding them that things have a way of working out.

When Jay Grelen read Little Grandmama's inscription in her Bible about tribulation, he says it was as though she had taken "pen in gentle hand and put it to paper, knowing that up the trail a ways, we, too, would need to know."

PUTTING IT INTO ACTION

1. What is God saying to grandparents in the following verses?

Deuteronomy 4:9—"Only take care, and keep your soul diligently, lest you forget the things that your eyes have seen, and lest they depart from your heart all the days of your life. Make them known to your children and your children's children."

Exodus 3:15—"God also said to Moses, 'Say this to the people of Israel: "The LORD, the God of your fathers, the God of Abraham, the God of Isaac, and the God of Jacob, has sent me to you." This is my name forever, and thus I am to be remembered throughout all generations.' "

Psalm 71:17-18—"O God, from my youth you have taught me, and I still proclaim your wondrous deeds. So even to old age and gray hairs, O God, do not forsake me, until I proclaim your might to another generation, your power to all those to come."

2. What is your faith and why is it important to you?

3. What are one or two ways you could encourage your grandchild to intentionally look for God's hand in life? For example, if you see a stunning sunset or sunrise with your granddaughter, you could remind her of the words of Psalm 19:1, "The heavens declare the glory of God, and the sky above proclaims his handiwork."

4. Jot down recollections of significant times when your faith caused you to take a defining path in your life.

- Choose one of these times to write about in detail. Briefly describe it below and also in *My Grandparenting Connection.*

- Commit to writing about this spiritual story by a certain date. Jot this date below and also write it in *My Grandparenting Connection.*

Chapter 7

Your Ancestors

One night our grandkids were playing the game Taboo with their parents. My daughter-in-law was trying to get the kids to guess the word "call." She described the word as "something you do on the phone."

The kids start jumping up and down while excitedly and confidently answering (in this order): "Play games!" No. "Text!" No. "Get on Facebook!" No.

Finally on attempt #4: "Call someone!" YES!!!

—Mary May Larmoyeux

By now, you've learned a lot about me. And I think I've learned something about you: You care about your one-of-a-kind grandchildren, and you want to connect with them in a way that joins you together heart-to-heart.

But here's something you don't know about me: It was only recently that I began to get really interested in my ancestors. My mother even asked me years ago if I wanted some genealogical things. I could kick myself now because I said no.

Younger then, it didn't matter to me who my great-great-great-great-great grandparents were. But that changed when I went to a genealogy conference, thinking some of the sessions would help me as a writer.

Instead, when I left that conference, I was changed, wanting to know about the family members who helped shape the person I am today.

More Than Names on a Family Tree

Ancestry is so much more than names on a family tree. Those names represent real people who had real strengths and weaknesses. Just ask Joanna Reed Shelton or Brenda Henry.

Joanna discovered something bigger than herself when she opened an email one day. It included an invitation to the 120th anniversary of a Japanese church founded by her great-grandfather, who was a Presbyterian missionary in the 19th century.

"When I read the email, I felt something pulling me toward Japan and the story of my great-grandfather's struggles and triumphs there," she said. "... His example would help launch my own journey of faith."[23]

And there's Brenda Henry who wrote about her family in *Searcy Living Magazine*. One of Brenda's grandfathers was the son of a Methodist preacher. "Grandpa might have known his Bible," Brenda said, "but to help support his family, he also knew

---

[23]"Finding Jesus in Japan," by Joanna Reed Shelton, *Christianity Today*, December 2016, 79-80.

how to make corn liquor. Mom said she always wondered why he grew so much corn and bought lots of sugar until he had to serve three months in jail, then she figured it out!"

Brenda described not only her grandfather but also her mother's life. "Mom made our clothes out of feed or flower sacks…Diapers were made out of torn up clothes, blankets, or any old material she could find."[24]

Delores' Dad

My friend Delores Bull describes below a snippet of what life was like for her as a child:

The first eight years of my life were spent in the country with loving parents and a younger sister, and doing all the fun things you could do on a farm.

My dad was stern in his discipline but tempered it with love and humor. His favorite threat for disobedience was, "I'll tear you up like a sow's bed." We found that so funny as all of our pigs slept in mud holes!

Every child dreams of a bicycle and my dream came true with a bright blue one purchased at a farm auction. Soon I was riding everywhere and not content to stay within my boundaries. I could see a steep hill not too far

---

[24]"Mom's Legacy," by Brenda Henry, *Searcy Living Magazine*, December 6, 2016, 78.

from our front yard and adventure began calling my name.

One afternoon my sister and I rode to the main road and pushed the bike to the top of the hill. With her safely secured on the handlebars, our flight began with our spirits soaring! But halfway down the hill, there was an altitude problem and the bike and its riders began to slide across the gravel road into a ditch. Our adventure was over and two bruised and battered little girls pushed a very battered blue bike toward home.

I can still feel the gentleness of my mother's hands as she cleaned and bandaged our many wounds. Sardines never snuggled any closer than my sister and me as we lay on that old divan.

Soon we heard the chug of the tractor as it pulled into the yard. With the slam of the screen door, we knew our dad was home and with eyes tightly closed, waited for punishment to begin. Instead, moments later we heard footsteps leaving the room.

Fifty years later, that incident was never mentioned between my dad and me. I know that many lessons have shaped my life. I learned not from what my father said, but from what he didn't say.

Don't details make a wonderful difference? They transform the family stories we write into living paintings for future generations, created with words.

Questions to Ask Your Older Relatives

I am an ultra-beginner when it comes to genealogy and family history, so please look to genealogical services and experts to be your ancestry guide. Also, ask your local librarian to suggest books about researching a family history. And check out your library for online genealogical databases it offers.

You may want to order a lecture series from The Great Courses® called *Discovering Your Roots: An Introduction to Genealogy* by John Philip Colletta, Ph.D. I listened to this, and it was extremely helpful!

Dr. Colletta gave tips for interviewing relatives that include making them feel comfortable, meeting in their home if possible, and showing them any kind of equipment you plan to use during the interview (digital recorder, camera, etc.).

He also said to ask specific questions and to phrase your questions from the viewpoint of your relative. For example, say, "What do you remember about your mother?" instead of "What do you remember about Nonnie?"

You might want to bring some kind of prompt such as an old family picture, a certificate of marriage, or a yellowed obituary. Also, ask your relative if they have a Bible with a listing of family marriages and births.

My mom was in her nineties when I interviewed her with a hand-held recorder. After I was finally able to explain why I wanted to ask her "all those questions," she readily shared what she recalled from the past.

What about you? Who are the oldest living relatives in your family? The types of questions you could ask them are endless, but here are a few ideas:

- When and where were you born?
- What was it like growing up?
- Tell me about your mom and dad: Where did they grow up? What did they look like? What were their occupations?
- How many brothers and sisters did they have? What were they like as children?
- Did you go to church as a child? If so, tell me about it.
- What was it like the day I was born?
- What do you want me to remember about you?
- Where did various pieces of "family furniture" come from?
- Bring pictures of family furniture on the interview. Also ask your relative to show you furniture that has special meaning to them. Then ask them why it is meaningful. Remember to take a picture of your relative by the special table, chair, etc.
- What did you learn from your grandparents about God?
- What is the most important thing you have learned about life?
- What role has faith played in your life?
- What was school like when you were growing up? Who was your favorite teacher?

After you have gathered information about your ancestor, write a description or biography.

Team Research with Your Grandchild

Your one-of-a-kind grandchild may want to do some genealogical research with you. Here are some possible topics you could address as a team:

- Research names on the family tree.
- Visit cemeteries where your ancestors are buried.
- Put together a scrapbook with old family pictures in it and identify the pictures with names, places, and dates if you know them.
- Examine records on the internet of church memberships and baptisms.
- Learn about your ancestors' occupations.
- Visit the obituaries of historical newspapers.
- Identify people in old family photographs.
- Interview the oldest family members together (you may want to videotape or record this). Take a picture with this relative. If possible, also take a picture of their home.
- Make a timeline of your ancestors' lives, beginning with the date of their birth. Ask your ancestors to jot on the timeline historical events they have experienced. Then ask them to tell you and your grandchild about one or two of these events.
- Encourage your grandchild to interview you about your life.

- Show your grandchild your high school or college yearbook.
- Tell your grandchildren about the day they were born.

Anne Dierks had fourteen grandchildren. And for more than a decade, she and her husband hosted what she called Granny Camp.[25]

The Dierks' grandchildren flew in once a year for the special camp. And one of their favorite activities was the teaching of Granddad's *G*'s—it included topics such as the Golden Rule, Goals, God, Grades, and yes...Genealogy.

Learning about ancestors can be a lot of fun for all generations!

When Rita's family gathers for the holidays, one of her nieces asks different questions about family members. For example, "Who asked her sister to catch her when she planned to slide down the slate roof on a blanket?" After everyone guesses, the name and picture of the correct relative is revealed.

PUTTING IT INTO ACTION

1. List your ancestors who are still living (continue on next page).

---

[25]*Granny Camp! How to Bond with Your Grandchild* by Anne Dierks, © 2010 by Anne C. Dierks, Published in 2010 by Cedar Mountain Books, LLC.

(continued from page 90))

2. Would you like to do some genealogical research with a grandchild? If so, which grandchild will you call first about this?

3. Look on the internet for genealogical sources. List two of these sources below.

4. Has your grandchild interviewed you about your life? If not, set a date for an interview. Write this date below, along with the name of the grandchild who will interview you.

Also write the date and the name in in *My Grandparenting Connection.*

5. Some questions were listed in this chapter under "Team Research with Your Grandchild." If your grandchild would like to do some genealogical research with you, choose one topic to begin exploring together. Write this topic below and also in *My Grandparenting Connection.*

Chapter 8

Your Treasured
Possessions

*What did my grandparents' house smell like? Mothballs!
That's because my grandparents had a very special rug in their
living room. Not wanting moths to damage it, Grandma
sprinkled mothballs on top of it!*

—John

When Beth Feeback walked into a North
Carolina Goodwill store, she was looking for
a blanket or afghan to keep her warm. But she left
with a throw, pair of gloves, and two large red,
white, and blue abstract paintings that she didn't
even like. Intending to paint over the canvasses, she
showed them first to a friend.

The friend spotted a Weatherspoon Art Gallery
label that identified one of the paintings as *Vertical
Diamond*,[26] by Ilya Bolotowsky. She suggested Beth

---

[26]"Painting Bought for $9.99 at Goodwill Valued at $15K,"
http://abcnewsradioonline.com/business-news/painting-bought-for-
999-at-goodwill-valued-at-15k.html, accessed on 4/21/19.

do some research before modifying the designs. Turns out that Bolotowsky was a notable twentieth century artist.

Five months after Beth walked into the Goodwill store, Sotheby's auctioned *Vertical Diamond* for $34,500.[27] Wouldn't you like to find such a treasure!

But how would you feel if the treasure meant to be passed down to your grandchildren or great-grandchildren was instead sold at a yard sale or second-hand store?

Jim and I have several rocking chairs, but the one I cherish most is crafted from heavy oak. More than forty years ago, I spotted it at a garage sale, but did not buy it then. The old chair had belonged to the grandmother of the person having the sale. She told me this when I bought one of her grandmother's old kerosene lamps.

A day or two later, after regretting my decision not to purchase the rocking chair, I called the woman who had the garage sale. She had given everything that had not sold to an auction house.

To make a long story short, I went to the auction and paid one dollar for the now cherished chair. That was probably the best buy I ever made. That old chair now holds so many personal memories! I have rocked our children and grandchildren in it,

---

[27]Vertical Diamond, http://www.sothebys.com/en/auctions/ecatalogue/2012/contemporary-art-n08875/lot.365.lotnum.html. Accessed on 4/29/19.

and hope one of our grandchildren will rock my great-grandchildren in it one day.

My friend Rita has her parents' rocking chair in her guest bedroom. When she has a problem, she goes to that familiar chair. She says, "I place my hands on the worn curves where my mother's and father's weathered hands rested from time to time."

And then she adds: "When my mother and I had tea, Dad sat in the chair. And when Dad and I looked at his tomato plants, Mom rocked in the chair. I often share this memory with our children and grandchildren."[28]

Yes, rocking chairs have many stories to tell. Just ask Sandra Marshall. She had to make some hard decisions when she moved into a smaller home.

Some of this stuff just has to be left behind because it won't fit. I'll take this rocking chair though. It has scars on the back from the kitten's claws and teeth marks on the arm from my grandson. I need it.

The rocking chair has given me a place to rest so many times—early morning devotions, late night teething sessions, Sunday afternoon visits with my grandmother, and watching sunsets all alone after my husband died.

Over and over again, God has wrapped His arms around me and rocked me gently to a realization that wherever I am in the world, He is with me, and He is enough.[29]

---

[28] Used with permission.
[29]"Do You Have a Favorite Rocking Chair?" https://legacyconnection.org/favorite-rocking-chair. Accessed on 4/29/19

Do you have a piece of furniture or a keepsake that means a lot to you? What memories does it bring to your mind? Have you told your grand-children about them?

Family Treasures

My friend Arlene Kirk has been intentional in capturing family memories associated with treasured family possessions. "If my kids could just hold on to the memory," she says, "the money is nothing."

In her den today hangs a beautiful picture of a barn in a weathered frame. And that frame was made from the very wood of her parents' barn. When her father no longer had milk cows, the barn became Arlene's playhouse.

The picture was taken the day her father was buried. "The sun was setting on the back of the silo," Arlene says.

A windowpane that was once in the "barn turned playhouse" now contains pictures from four different periods of Arlene and her husband's life. Its four panes contain photos of their parents and grandparents, Wayne and Arlene's children with their aunts and uncles, Wayne and Arlene raising their three children, and their grandchildren.

Now married more than sixty years, Arlene passes down the stories of possessions that mean a lot to her. She does this in everyday life. "Through the years we will pull something out to use, and I'll say, 'That was my grandmother's.'"

"The memory is what is important to pass on," says Arlene.

Her oldest granddaughter is already getting sentimental about things that have been passed down in her family. Arlene thinks that's a good thing and says, "She needs a history in her life, too."

Like Arlene, passing down family history is important to me. And some of my most precious possessions are the Bibles I've had over the years. Not only for the truth they contain but also for the memories they hold. For more than two decades I have recorded joys and sorrows, births and deaths...the answers God gave to so many prayers.

One day my daughter-in-law, Tonya, called, saying she was trying to remember all of the things God had done for her. She knows I keep a running list in my Bible of answered prayers, so in no time I was able to tell her what I found—a record of God's faithfulness.

The list included the dates of the grandkids' baptisms...buying and selling of houses...times that God intervened in amazing ways. An example was a notation made in November 2004: "God protected Chris from a terrible wreck when he did a 360-degree spin on a wet freeway and went into a ditch."

Another notation, dated May 2011, said Tonya's van had somehow caught on fire when she was on the freeway with the kids. I wrote in my Bible, "Praise the Lord for protecting them and providing help!"

Antiques Roadshow

More than fifty years ago, I pretended to be royalty when sitting in a tall wooden chair in my grandparents' house. It was my "Queen Chair." I now have that chair, and it means a lot to me. I would never sell it because it reminds me of my Nana. But I wondered about its value.

That's why Jim and I brought it to the *Antiques Roadshow* when it came to Little Rock. After waiting in a long line, we wove ourselves around to the furniture appraiser.

First, a middle-aged man asked about the history of the chair. Then he flipped it over and examined the bottom of the seat. He spotted what looked like a fading label and on it there was some type of signature.

I took a deep breath as the appraiser took out a magnifying glass and attempted to read it.

A few seconds later, he said the chair was made of oak, it was of good quality. It was indeed about 100 years old. But it had been manufactured, not made by hand, in the early twentieth century. And the estimated value was $150.

Yes, $150. Not $1,000, $5,000 or more.

After first feeling a bit let down, I remembered: The best things in life don't have price tags. The Queen Chair had not deflated in worth that day. Its value never changed.

To me, it was, and still is, priceless! I hope that my great-great grandchildren will sit in it one day.

Heirlooms to Pass Down to Future Generations

When I touch something that belonged to a great-grandparent or grandparent, I feel like I'm connecting my legacy to theirs. And, I guess I really am.

But what about you? Do you have a prized family possession to pass down to your grandchildren? Other than vintage chairs and tattered Bibles, you might want to consider old photographs, clocks, watches, letters, diaries, jewelry, toys, collections, a cherished rocking chair...a quilt.

Do your children and grandchildren know what you treasure and why?

PUTTING IT INTO ACTION

1. If you have pieces of family furniture, list them below:

2. If you have pieces of furniture that have been passed down through the generations, take pictures of these items and write the family history that goes with them. If possible, attach an envelope on the back of the heirloom with its family history (who owned it, any special memories with it, etc.).

3. With your grandchild, visit relatives who have pieces of furniture that are family heirlooms. Together, chronicle some of the history of the furniture. When will you do this?

4. It's been said that baby boomers treasure personal keepsakes and family stories more than money.[30] Is it time to ask your children and adult grandchildren which of your family possessions they would like to have one day?

If so, who will you talk with first? When will you have this conversation? Answer below and also in *My Grandparenting Connection.*

---

[30]"Your heirs want this even more than your money," by Andrea Coombes, 12/31/13. https://www.marketwatch.com/story/your-heirs-want-this-even-more-than-your-money-2013-12-16. Market Watch. Accessed on 3/14/19.

Chapter 9

Your Family Photographs

I could not find a good parking space when I was taking my three-year-old granddaughter to lunch. Then a car suddenly pulled out of a space near the front door and I mumbled to myself, "Thank you, Jesus, for this amazing parking space." To that my granddaughter replied, "Mare Mare, that's not Jesus! That's a lady old like you driving that car!"[31]

—Marilyn Conley

Several years ago, Jim and I bought an antique oval frame at a flea market. We purchased it for a large family picture.

The oval frame enclosed a black and white picture of perhaps a ten-month-old girl. She was sitting on a short stool in what looked like a white christening gown. Ever since we bought that frame, I've wondered about the little girl's story.

The aging photograph has an inscription on the back that's very difficult to read. It definitely looks

---

[31]"Kids Say the Funniest Things," accessed April 20, 2019, https://legacyconnection.org/kids-say-the-funniest-things. Used with permission.

like the year 1812 and a name that is hard to pinpoint—maybe Charlotte Prindle—or Prindle Charlotte—or Prindle Charlotte Marsh. I asked a genealogist how I could identify the large photo. He discounted my question because photographs were not even taken in the year 1812. But I still wonder, who was she?

How could a once prized picture now be hidden by my family's generational photograph? Was it placed in the wooden frame by a loving parent or grandparent? It's unlikely that anyone living today knows that answer, but there is one thing for sure. Baby Prindle's picture is not where it belongs.

So how did it get to a flea market?

Just think about it. Have you ever seen old pictures in estate sales, antique stores, or weekend garage sales? Maybe black and white photographs of radiant brides, cooing babies, or grandpas with long beards.

Once cherished, they were tossed aside to be sold for mere pennies. Or even worse, many old pictures are simply thrown away with the weekly trash. I don't want that to happen to my family's pictures.

But if something happened to Jim and me now, our children do not have the time to sort through my boxes of videos, audiotapes, and pictures...not to mention the thousands of photos on the computer and the countless stories they tell.

Those pictures represent the family roots of great-great grandchildren I will never see. And they will never see those pictures if I do not preserve them.

Every Picture Tells a Story

Have you ever discovered a family picture, wishing you knew much more about it? Many years ago, when I was looking through some old photographs with my mother, my eye caught a picture of a little girl being held by a young woman. They were standing by an old table that Jim and I now have.

Curious about the story behind that image, I asked Mom to tell me about it. Turns out it was taken when Mom was a little girl. Her mother—my grandmother—was holding her. And the table was set for her fourth birthday party!

Well, Mom gave that picture to me and today it hangs on a wall in my house—near the very table where my mother celebrated her fourth birthday. And sometimes when I touch that table, I think of my grandmother and my mother. The old table has many stories to tell, but I only know of the one in the picture.

So how do we begin to capture the many stories behind our cherished photos? Karen Jordan suggests that we begin with these steps:[32]

People. Can you identify the people within the shot? If not, do you know anyone who can? Can you write a description of that person? Who else might have been around when the shot was taken?

---

[32]"Because Every Photo Tells a Story," accessed 3/27/19, karenjordan.net/every-photo-tells-a-story. Used with permission.

Places. Do you know where the picture was taken? Can you describe the place at that time? Do you know anything about the history of the area? And what do you know about the area now?

Time. When was the shot taken? What time period? What was going on in the world at that time? What changes have taken place since that time?

Events. Do you know what event was taking place when the photo was taken? Can you tell what season of the year it was taken? What events might have been happening around that time?

Story. Does the picture remind you of a story? What came to mind as you thought about the people, places, or event that might have been taking place when the photo was shot.

Questions. You might think of even more questions you need to ask yourself about the photo that would help you capture an important family story.

Brainstorm. Take a moment and jot down your thoughts about your picture. You could include the picture when you preserve your story—in a scrapbook, on your computer, on a blog, in a notebook...the possibilities are endless!

What are some of your favorite family pictures? Why do you cherish them? I immediately think of three pictures: my parents' wedding picture, one of my father-in-law after World War II, and a baby picture of my older son, who only weighed three and a half pounds when he was born.

Each of these images captures one moment in the story of my family, and they also tell personal tales of the ups and downs of life.

Yes, stories of young love and a new husband going off to war, stories of devotion in sickness and sorrow, and stories of a baby's struggle to survive. They tell about ways God has worked in my family. Many times, what I once perceived as the worst thing possible set my life in a new, better direction.

But no one will know those stories, or even the names of the people in those pictures, if I do not do something about that today. My cherished picture could wind up like "Baby Prindle" someday.

My dear friend Rita, mother of six children, grandmother of fourteen, and great-grandmother of eleven, once told me, "We all have stories to tell. My time is running out, but I am working on it."

And my time is running out, too. That's why I am making an effort now to not only connect with each of my grandchildren, but also to somehow connect through family pictures and save their stories for generations I will never see.

Pictures: Some Things I've Done Right

Even though I have a long way to go when it comes to chronicling my family pictures, I have done some things right:

- Taken lots of pictures, especially at special events and family gatherings.
- Made individual albums for our children for the first twelve or so years of their lives.
- Captured everyday memories with those I love.
- Created hardback photo books, using an online photo service. The one I gave Mom on her ninetieth birthday was my favorite. It chronicled her life and legacy.
- Gave mom a digital photo frame with generational pictures in it.
- Made a family recipe book and included family pictures.
- Made annual photo calendars, giving one to each adult child as a Christmas gift.
- Asked our children to give us pictures of their families for Christmas.
- Realized my family's history is always changing. Because of this I have taken pictures to capture significant events. For example, when President Ronald Reagan visited Arkansas long ago, Jim and I brought our young boys to see him. We took pictures of our children in that crowd.

    And when we heard Holocaust survivor Agi Geva share about her war experiences, we had a picture taken with her. With an outstretched arm, she showed her concentration camp identification number.

- Brought some old pictures to our last family reunion and let our children and others take the ones they wanted to keep.

Pictures: Some of the Many Things I've Done Wrong

And I've done so many things wrong:

- Used self-adhesive magnetic scrapbooks when our children were small, and now many of the pictures in them are stuck to the pages.
- Took pictures of everything, and I mean everything, resulting in a mountain of uncategorized pictures today.
- Did not write names on the back of most of the pictures.
- Did not describe what was happening in pictures.
- Too often I did not ask Mom about old pictures, and now it's too late to ask her.
- Did not ask my grandparents about pictures and movies they had.
- Have no centralized place for family pictures—they are in scrapbooks, under the bed, in closets…
- Put important pictures in special places when we moved. Now, I have to find them.

So, what's someone like me to do about their stacks of photographs and electronic images?

When visiting the home of my friend Arlene, I asked her about this. It seems like all of her pictures have a story to tell.

She looked at a photograph hanging on her wall of an old windmill. "That windmill was in my mother and daddy's pasture," she said, "They would bring the cattle home for the winter to take care of them and they would have cattle drives to drive those cattle back up there. You did not use the farming land for cattle."

And then I spotted a picture of some children. "That silly picture?" she said, "Those are our six grandchildren, and they love to do something different when they come over."

Arlene is in the process of sorting through all of her old pictures and giving them to her children and grandchildren. She's dividing what she has unless she has a picture that everyone wants. Then she makes a duplicate.

She's also sorting her digital pictures into folders on her computer. And when her family has its reunion every three years, she puts the pictures in a digital photo frame for all to enjoy.

"I need to put names on the back of the pictures," she says, "so the kids will know their distant cousins. If we don't do this, we have lost our heritage."

PUTTING IT INTO ACTION

Circle one of the ideas on the following list that you would like to begin. Then write it in *My Grandparenting Connection.*

- Take a general inventory of your family pictures. Are they preserved in scrapbooks, stored in boxes on a shelf, or kept as digital images on your cell phone or computer?

- Ask your siblings and older relatives to show you the family pictures they have. Make copies of those you want in your collection.

- Select fifty of your favorite pictures and write names and descriptions on the back. Put a sticky note on any that need to be duplicated for multiple children or grandchildren.

- Do you know the names of your ancestors? If possible, scan their pictures and put them in a family tree for future generations.

- Do you have a child who was named after a family member or special friend? If so, on the back of the namesake's picture, jot why their particular name was chosen. Give that picture to a now adult child.

- If possible, gather pictures of the homes where your parents, grandparents, and great-grandparents lived. Write a favorite memory or two on the back of these pictures.

- Do you have pictures of your grandchildren that were taken on the day they were born? Put them in a frame and jot on the back of the pictures the names and a few of your thoughts and feelings that day. You may even want to write a short prayer for each grandchild's life and sign your name.

- Read a book about preserving family photographs or one about using photographs to discover your ancestry.
- Make a slideshow of family pictures and show them at your next family reunion. Or, put them in a digital picture frame and bring it to the next family reunion.

Chapter 10

Your Life Lessons
from Successes, Failures,
Struggles, and Regrets

The road to success and the road to failure are almost exactly the same.

—Colin R. Davis

A grandson asked me how old I'll be when he's a teenager. The truth is, I'll be about the age that my grandmother was when she entered eternity. Of course, I didn't tell him that. I think I said something like, "old."

But his question made me think, *How many years do I have left on Earth, and how does God want me to use them?* So I've renewed my vow to get the countless scrapbooks in order and to write down more of our family's stories.

Although I love to jot down uplifting family stories, it's often painful to recall those with struggles and failures. And yet, isn't life filled with many disappointments? If we do not let our grandchildren have a peek into the challenges we face, how will they know how to handle their own?

In the last chapter, I mentioned three of my favorite pictures: Mom and Dad when they married, Jim's dad after World War II, and our firstborn son. Each one not only tells of triumph but also underlying stories of heartache and doubt. Let's look at each of these pictures.

Would Dad Come Home?

The wedding photo of Mom and Dad was taken before my father, who was in the Navy, was shipped off to war. My parents must have been filled with both joy and fear of the unknown as they married.

The photo I have is a copy of their only wedding picture. The story goes that Mom's parents gave them money to get multiple wedding pictures made. But Mom and Dad decided to just get one photo taken and use the rest of the money to celebrate. Years ago, Mom said she wished she and Dad had made a different choice then.

How many times have you had fears about tomorrow? How often have you been shortsighted and made the wrong choice? If you are like me, many!

And then there's the picture of my father-in-law sitting in a wheelchair at an Army-Navy football game. Jim and I stumbled across it a few years ago. Although I knew Jim's dad had been wounded in World War II, the seriousness of his injuries had not sunk in.

That changed when I saw the photo of "The Major" sitting in a wheelchair in a special sidelines section of the football game. His leg was propped up, and he was surrounded by others recovering from war injuries.

Before the war, my father-in-law had planned to become a doctor. But after the war, his plans changed. Instead he became a high school chemistry teacher and prepared many students for the profession he once dreamed of.

And there's the picture of our oldest son who was born two months early. When Jim and I married, we never thought we'd see a child of ours struggle for life. Never imagined doctors saying they did not expect our firstborn to survive.

But God had other plans. Now a husband and father, Chris has a strong faith and a beautiful family. His children know how God intervened in a desperate situation and answered prayers.

Connecting with Your Grandchild

Billy Graham said, "Don't be bound by the past and its failures. But don't forget its lessons either."[33]

What about you? What trials have you gone through? How have you seen them turned around for good? Psalm 78:4 (NIV) says: "...we will tell the next generation the praiseworthy deeds of the LORD, his power, and the wonders he has done."

---

[33] "In His Own Words: Billy Graham on Encouragement," https://billygrahamlibrary.org/in-his-own-words-billy-graham-on-encouragement. Accessed March 29, 2019.

And the Bible paraphrase *The Message* says it this way (Psalm 78:4): "...I'll let you in on the sweet old truths, stories we heard from our fathers, counsel we learned at our mother's knee. We're not keeping this to ourselves, we're passing it along to the next generation—God's fame and fortune, the marvelous things he has done."

When a grandchild tells you about her wonderful new best friend, first listen. Then, tell her something about your best friend when you were her age.

When a grandchild tells you about being hurt by a friend, first listen. Then tell him about a time when a friend disappointed you.

If a grandchild loses an election at school, wins a race, moves to a new city, grieves over their parents' divorce, becomes pregnant out of wedlock...can you identify? Maybe, maybe not. But you can listen and care and pray. Depending on their age, you can tell them of your struggles and how you found hope.

Scott Williams, a writer for FamilyLife, said:

As painful as it is, we need to let our children fail sometimes. Failure is a good teacher, and God is a redeeming God. Don't seek to cocoon them from life's bumps and bruises. Coach them through challenges and difficulties. Don't do all the heavy lifting for them.

Teach them diligence and perseverance, the value of doing their best, and then let them do it themselves. Cheer

114

them on in their successes, and be there with unconditional love when they fail.[34]

Those are good words for a parent and grandparent. We need to be there for our children and grandchildren and point them to God. When things seem hopeless to your grandchild, tell them of times when life looked hopeless to you, too.

My guess is that my father-in-law's life looked pretty hopeless when he lay on a battlefield in Holland, wondering if he would survive. But survive he did. And by God's grace, and countless surgeries, he went on to be a high school Hall of Fame chemistry teacher. His legacy lives on.

What tales of triumphs and tragedies does God want you to share with the next generation?

Seven Ways to Pass on Lessons About the Ups and Downs of Life

One of the best ways to remind your grandchild that God is in control, is to tell them about your life experiences. Help them cling to the truth of Romans 8:28, "And we know that for those who love God all things work together for good, for those who are called according to his purpose."

---

[34] "Lessons From the College Admissions Scandal," Accessed April 21, 2019. https://www.familylife.com/articles/topics/parenting/essentials/releasing-your-child/lessons-from-the-college-admissions-scandal. Used with permission.

Now this does not mean things will always work out in the way we want. Often God has plans that simply do not make sense to us. We think in terms of the here and now. His focus is eternity.

Here are seven ways you can help your grandchild trust God:

1. Talk about your **successes, failures, struggles, and regrets** in everyday life—while you are washing the dishes, preparing a Thanksgiving feast, going on a hike. Be intentional about looking for natural opportunities to teach life lessons to your grandchildren.

If you have a family reunion, schedule a special time when loved ones can share about the various twists and turns of their lives.

2. Identify pictures that chronicle some of your high and low points. Talk with older grandchildren about what God taught you during that phase of your life.

3. What **historical events** have you lived through? For example, the assassination of John F. Kennedy, the Vietnam War, the death of Elvis Presley, the resignation of President Richard Nixon, integration of public schools, the introduction of computers and cell phones, September 11 attacks, Watergate, a hurricane, a tornado, a political rally…a pro-life march. The list could go on and on.

Have you talked with your grandkids about how your life changed with these events?

116

4. Ask your older relatives about your family. What stories do they remember about your parents...about "Uncle Joe"? Do they have family pictures or movies? What are some of the ups and downs they have experienced in life?

5. Tell your grandchildren **what you have learned** through your ups and downs of life. Jot down life events you've experienced: marriage, birth of a child, separation or divorce, choosing a profession, leaving friends because of moving to a new country...a new city...a new house, loss of a child, miscarriage, adoption, foster care, taking care of a mother- or father-in-law when they became old...debilitating sickness or injury, loss of a job, major disagreement with a close friend, spiritual milestones, when faith became real to you...Again, the list could go on and on.

6. Spend time thinking about things that happened in your life that you once considered bad, but now can see **how they worked for good.** Jot down a list of these times and share this list with your grandchildren.

7. If **your parents** are living, ask them about historical events they have experienced and what they learned through them. Bring a grandchild with you, and record what your parents say.

Looking Back

My parents are gone from this Earth now, but I think of them often. When I see a picture of them, I remember their perseverance in the life's challenges.

I can see the reflection of my mother when I look in a mirror. And I think of her when I eat oatmeal the "healthy" way, with butter and brown sugar. But most importantly, when I am going through a very hard time in life, I can almost hear her whispering from heaven, "Mary, things have a way of working out."

While Mom was living, she said that phrase over and over and over again. Now that I have lived so many years, I hear the ring of truth in those very words, and I understand.

How often I forget that eyes and ears of children and grandchildren are watching and listening. We have lessons to tell. Experiences to share. Heart connections to make so they, too, will know that things have a way of working out.

PUTTING IT INTO ACTION

1. Make a chronological list of historical events you have experienced (continue on next page):

(continued from page 118)

Which one of these historical events will you discuss first with your grandchild? Write your answer below and also in *My Grandparenting Connection.*

2. Make two lists of turning points in your life:

- Your successes:

- Your failures, struggles, and regrets:

3. Choose one thing from each list of turning points that you would like to talk about with your grandchild. Write these two things below and also in *My Grandparenting Connection.* (Include an estimated discussion date. Consider your grandchild's age and what they are going through when making your choices.)

Chapter 11

Your Unconditional Love

When a grandson was in kindergarten, he said he loved his teacher. He wanted to marry her one day because "she's nice, wears pretty clothes, and gives me three chances."

—Mary May Larmoyeux

More than ten years ago, when Jim and I were visiting our grandkids' school for its Grandparents Day celebration, the highlight was a visit to the kindergarten class. The teacher gave each grandparent a list of things the children said about them. Here's a sampling:

- Grandmas and grandpas are older than mothers and fathers and like to hold grandchildren in their laps and hug them.
- They like to answer questions.
- When they read to us, they don't skip words, and they never care if we ask for the same story over again.
- They don't say hurry up.
- They usually have lots of quarters.

- They don't have to do anything except be there when we come see them.
- They shouldn't play hard or run.
- They especially like to read stories to grandchildren from big books with lots of pictures.

Don't you just love the innocence and simplicity of a child? "Grandma always made you feel she had been waiting to see just you all day," Marcy DeMaree said, "and now the day was complete."

Going to see Great-Grandma

Who comes to your mind when you think of unconditional love? For me, it's my mother. I well remember what happened when our grandson Cade visited her after he got a new haircut. He was eight years old at the time.

About a week before the visit, Cade asked his mom if he could get a mohawk. If you aren't familiar with that hairstyle, both sides of the head are shaved and a strip of obviously longer hair stands straight up in the center. Yes, straight up!

Cade's mother asked her Facebook friends how she should deal with this. One said it was a sign that Cade would be rebellious and that this spirit needed to be nipped in the bud. Others thought it was just a funny little-kid idea.

Not wanting to be the bad guy, Tonya decided to defer to good ole dad. So I breathed a sigh of relief, believing he'd say something like, "You are eight years old, the answer is no."

But that's not what happened. When Cade asked his dad about the haircut, his father asked him to explain why he wanted a mohawk. If I remember correctly Cade said something like he thought it would look "cool."

And his dad said, "Okay."

"Okay?" What was my son thinking? Especially since Cade would visit his great-grandmother in a few days. She's from the era of women wearing white gloves and no facial hair for men, much less a mohawk on her first great-grandson.

Yes, Cade got his haircut. But he changed his mind about the style. Instead of a mohawk, he got a reverse mohawk—he had a shaved strip right down the middle of his head. Could things get any worse?

Well, Cade went to see Great Grandma, and his parents videotaped her reaction. It was not what I had expected. She squealed and had a huge smile. Then she laughed and said something like, "Isn't that cute!"

My mother did not care what Cade looked like. She loved him unconditionally.

Surprisingly, just a few days after Cade's visit to see his great-grandmother, he had a whole new hairstyle. Turns out that he didn't like the reverse mohawk. He shaved it off himself.

Wise Words

Of course, the challenges we face with kids and grandkids are usually more significant than a hairstyle. Sometimes a child or grandchild will turn their back on God.

Andrew Palau, son of evangelist Luis Palau, is an evangelist himself today. But he did not always follow the Lord. When he was about thirteen years old, he loved to party. He had a reputation as being a wild kid. He liked to drink and smoke marijuana.

Andrew's parents realized they could not convince him to change his ways. So they sought biblical counsel and prayed. And prayed...and prayed. "We showed him as much love I think as parents can ever show a guy,"[35] said his father, Luis.

But it was not until Andrew was twenty-seven that he became a changed person—a follower of Jesus Christ.

Have you been praying for a wayward grandchild? Do you seldom see a grandchild because of divorce? Like Andrew's parents, don't give up. Jesus said in John 14:1, "Let not your hearts be troubled. Believe in God; believe also in me."

When things look hopeless, lean on God; trust that He is working in your grandchild's life. Know that only God has the full understanding of things.

In *The Hiding Place*, Corrie ten Boom told a story that helps us comprehend the meaning of trusting contentment:

And so seated next to my father in the train compartment, I suddenly asked, "Father, what is sexsin?"

---

[35] "My Parents Kept Praying While I Kept Partying," by Andrew Palau, https://www.familylife.com/articles/topics/real-stories/parenting-real-stories/my-parents-kept-praying-while-i-kept-partying. Accessed 3/29/19.

He turned to look at me, as he always did when answering a question, but to my surprise he said nothing. At last he stood up, lifted his traveling case off the floor and set it on the floor.

"Will you carry it off the train, Corrie?" he said.

I stood up and tugged at it. It was crammed with the watches and spare parts he had purchased that morning.

"It's too heavy," I said.

"'Yes," he said, "and it would be a pretty poor father who would ask his little girl to carry such a load. It's the same way, Corrie, with knowledge. Some knowledge is too heavy for children. When you are older and stronger, you can bear it. For now, you must trust me to carry it for you."[36]

Perhaps you are going through a difficult time with a grandchild. Maybe your family worries seem too heavy. If so, say and believe a "helpless prayer." As Corrie ten Boom learned, there are times when only God is able to carry our burdens.

Yes, God is always working in ways we may never see. And while He is changing hearts, he wants each of us to love our grandchildren unconditionally. Do your grandchildren know you will always be there for them? That your love for them is not based on whether they succeed or fail?

---

[36] Material taken from *The Hiding Place* © 1971, Corrie ten Boom and John and Elizabeth Sherrill, used by permission of Barbour Publishing, Inc.

Words to Ponder

My friend Rita told me a precious story about her great-grandson when he was eleven years old. He had a class assignment to write about his family, and he wrote the following about their love:

> *Think of love as water. It carries you through the raging torrent, and then becomes peaceful. This proves that love is everlasting like a stream of water. Like the stream turns into a river, love grows larger and larger. Then the stream goes underground and after thousands of years it makes crystal and then …diamond. An unbreakable jewel most treasured by few, just like love.*[37]

What a deep understanding this boy had about the most precious gift: unconditional love.

Rita also wrote a beautiful poem about unconditional love. Think of your grandchild as you read it.

You Are Not Alone
by Rita Goodgame

Listen to the soft breath of a child
whose warm head rests upon your chest.
Listen to your own words of affection.
"You are special."
"You are not alone."
"Cherish the desire to become the person

---

[37] Used with permission.

you are meant to be."
"I will love you forever."

Listen to earth sounds…wind sounds…rain sounds
… whispers…bell sounds…prayer sounds…lullabies
…birdsong…laughter…melodies…a baby's heartbeat.
Listen to the sounds of God's creatures in His
universe.

Listen, breathe deeply, dream sweet dreams
and listen again.

"You are loved."[38]

Does your grandchild know that nothing they can ever do or say could remove your love? Do they believe that you do not love them more when they win or lose the race? When they visit your home, do they believe you don't have anything more important to do that day than seeing them?

Have you ever thought of your unconditional love as an unbreakable jewel?

PUTTING IT INTO ACTION

1. First Corinthians 13: 3-7 from the Bible para-phrase *The Message* says:

If I give everything I own to the poor and even go to the stake to be burned as a martyr, but I don't love, I've

---

[38]"Listen" by Rita Goodgame, accessed March 29, 2019.
https://legacyconnection.org/listen. Used with permission.

gotten nowhere. So, no matter what I say, what I believe, and what I do, I'm bankrupt without love.

Love never gives up.
Love cares more for others than for self.
Love doesn't want what it doesn't have.
Love doesn't strut,
Doesn't have a swelled head,
Doesn't force itself on others,
Isn't always "me first,"
Doesn't fly off the handle,
Doesn't keep score of the sins of others,
Doesn't revel when others grovel,
Takes pleasure in the flowering of truth,
Puts up with anything,
Trusts God always,
Always looks for the best,
Never looks back,
But keeps going to the end.

2. Spend a few minutes thinking of how God and others have shown you unconditional love. Now consider how you express love to your grandchild. Jot a few of your thoughts below.

3. Could you do something differently to help your unique grandchild sense your unconditional love? Write this below and also in *My Grandparenting Connection.*

128

Chapter 12

Your Family Recipes

Food is love. My mother took pride in feeding our family, always tried to make it fun, always made it fresh and hot.[39]

—Jennifer Garner

Not too long ago my oldest granddaughter and I made a batch of "Mamoo's Sugar Cookies." We used the very recipe that my mother taught me...the one her mother taught her almost 100 years ago. To our family, those simple cookies are much more than a sweet taste. They convey precious reminders of family and love.

I asked my Facebook friends if they have any special food memories with their grandparents or grandkids. Here's what a few of them said.

- "My grandma would let me make one biscuit for myself in a very small cast iron skillet. I

---

[39]"Farm Girl at Heart," introduction and interview by Krissy Tiglias, *Southern Living*, September 2018, 83.

have that skillet. The biscuits were home-made." – Vicki

- "I treasure the memory of my precious great-grandmother and her warm, rich blackberry cobbler." – Mary Ann
- "My grandmother let me cook with her. We especially loved making rice crispy treats." – Carolyn
- "I cannot think of most good homemade recipes without thinking of my Nanny. She was an awesome cook, and tried to cheer…console…and love us so many times by way of food." – Cassie
- "My grandmother would give us the leftover crust, and we would put cinnamon and sugar on it and bake it." – Andie

When you think of family recipes, what memories do you recall? Perhaps memories of a beloved grandmother or great-grandmother—the touch of her hand, the sound of her voice, the smell of homemade sugar cookies or hot apple pie.

I've never forgotten a particular conversation with one of our granddaughters. She and her little brother had spent the weekend with Pops and me, and one of the things that we did together was make a cake.

When our son and his wife came to pick up the children, we all ate lunch together. Of course, we had the kids' cake for dessert.

Our son said the cake tasted especially good. "Know why?" his three-year-old daughter asked. "I poured the cake mix in with all of my love," she said. "The goodness you taste is my love."

I think there's a lot of wisdom in what my granddaughter said that day. When we cook for family and friends, it's often much more than providing nutrition.

Food Memories

Author John Rosemond said that families are not made strong by money or material things. But instead by "that ineffable thing called love. Love is both expressed and strengthened when a family does things together, things that create traditions and positive memories."[40]

And almost anything can become a cherished family tradition says author Florence Littauer and her daughters Marita and Lauren. "Start with something that appeals to the majority," they say. "Maybe that's sharing cinnamon rolls together (homemade or store bought, it doesn't matter) the first Saturday morning of every month." [41]

Do you have family memories that revolve around food?

---

[40]"Family is strengthened one memory at a time," by John Rosemond. *Arkansas Democrat-Gazette*, January 8, 2003, 3E. Accessed February 12, 2019.

[41]*Making the Blue Plate Special* by Florence Littauer, Marita Littauer, and Lauren Littauer. Published 2006 by David C. Cook, 116.

When I was a little girl, we often went to the cafeteria after church on Sunday with my grandparents. There were five children in my family, and I remember a little game we played—who can spend the least amount for their lunch? I could get a stuffed pepper back then for $.39 – yes, thirty-nine cents!

And if my memory serves me correctly (and it might not), it seems like I was usually the "winner." Of course, as an adult, I now know what my smart parents were doing.

Other friends of mine have fond memories of family get-togethers on Sundays for lunch. LaRue's family all "crowded around the table, talking, laughing."

Hallie said her Granny Tolley cooked for all of her kids and grandkids every Saturday and Sunday! "The entire dining room table would be covered with at least ten dishes of food, fried chicken, mashed taters, deviled eggs, homemade rolls, and more!"

And when Arlene was growing up her family had dinners at Grandma's house and *everyone* came!

I doubt the grandparents of LaRue, Hallie, and Arlene thought their Sunday meals would be remembered as expressions of love. But they were.

Rita was surprised one Mother's Day when her son called telling her of a fond food memory. He wanted to make her cream puff recipe for his boys. "When I was about five years old," he said, "we went to the store, bought a certain kind of flour (cake flour) made a special recipe that rose like muffins, and we put custard inside and sprinkled powdered sugar on top. Where can I find that recipe and that flour?"

"Isn't it great that our children remember such events?" Rita said.

American actress Susan Strasberg sums up what many of us know about our grandparents' homes, "I loved their home, everything smelled older, worn but safe; the food aroma had baked itself into the furniture."[42]

Nine Ways to Pass On Family Recipes

1. Enlist your grandchild's help when making family recipes. Tell them about the origin of the recipe and why it's special to you.

2. Make a family recipe book (possibly recruit family members to help you put this together). Include who made the original recipe. If possible, have a picture of this person and a little biographical information. And if you have old handwritten recipes, scan them for the recipe book.

3. Frame a handwritten recipe, stains and all. Identify the loved one who jotted down this recipe and include a memory of making the recipe.

---

[42]www.bitsofpositivity.com/best-grandparent-quotes-including-grandmother-grandfather-quotes. Accessed November 9, 2019.

4. During family reunions, include at least one meal with favorite family recipes. Share the recipes with loved ones.

5. Intentionally make family foods at certain times of the year. An often-requested fall dessert in my family is Pumpkin Pie Cake. It's been made for many a birthday celebration and Thanksgiving dessert. (You can find this recipe at the end of this chapter.)

6. Frame a picture of a grandparent and grandchild making a family recipe together. Be sure to date the photograph and identify those in it.

7. Preserve handwritten recipes in a recipe keepsake binder. Many of these binders have clear pages for recipe cards. They can be found at many craft stores and on the internet.

8. Purposely plan regular family meals packed with good food and love. Put away the cell phones. Talk and laugh as you learn about each other's week.

9. Begin new traditions with recipes. Teach your grandchild how to make one (or more) of your own homemade recipes. You may want to shop together for the ingredients. Take a picture of the two of you making this recipe. Also, make it often when your grandchild visits.

Two Family Recipes from My Family to Yours

Earlier in this chapter, I mentioned the following family recipes. Enjoy!

Mamoo's Sugar Cookies*

1 cup butter
2 cups sugar
4 eggs
5 cups flour
4 tsp. baking powder
2 or more tsp. vanilla
Milk as needed

- Cream butter with sugar. Then add eggs.
- Sift flour and baking powder and add.
- Finally, add vanilla (and milk if needed).
- Form a roll with the dough, refrigerate for an hour or so, and then slice; OR chill dough and then roll out and cut dough into shapes.
- Add colored sugar, sprinkles, etc., before baking. Bake at 350 degrees for about 10-12 minutes.

*Note: This recipe does not require salt.

Pumpkin Pie Cake

4 eggs slightly beaten
1 sixteen-ounce can pumpkin
1 ½ cup sugar
2 tsp. pumpkin pie spice
1 tsp. salt
1 can evaporated milk (13 oz.)
1 box yellow cake mix
1 cup chopped nuts
2 sticks margarine (for baking)

- Mix the first **six ingredients** together and then pour into ungreased 9 x 13 pan.
- Sprinkle the yellow cake mix on top of this.
- Melt the margarine and pour it on top of the mixture.
- Add chopped nuts.
- Bake at 350 degrees for 1½ hours.

Sometimes we top a piece of hot Pumpkin Pie Cake with Cool Whip or vanilla ice cream. Delicious!

PUTTING IT INTO ACTION

1. Do you have a prized recipe that your mother or grandmother used to make? What is it and when will you teach your grandchild how to make it?

2. What is one of your favorite family recipes? Why did you choose this recipe? Write your answers below and also in *My Grandparenting Connection*.

3. Ask your grandchild to help you select a menu to prepare for the family. If your grandchild does not live nearby, plan this for their next visit. Write some of your ideas about this below.

4. Choose one or two recipe ideas that you would like to use. Write them below and also in *My Grandparenting Connection.*

Chapter 13

Your Holiday and Birthday Traditions

When one of our grandkids heard that Jesus was born of a virgin, he said, "I didn't know Jesus was born in Virginia."

—Mary May Larmoyeux

"Family is strengthened one memory at a time,"[43] said parenting author John Rosemond. And what better time to create one-of-a-kind memories than Christmas, Thanksgiving, Easter, and birthdays?

A few years ago, when I was giving grandkids some ornaments to hang on the Christmas tree, my mind wandered back to my childhood.

As a little girl, my parents always had our Christmas tree in the living room. Mom sat on the couch, adding hooks to the ornaments. Then she handed an ornament to my brother, three sisters,

---

[43] "Family is strengthened one memory at a time," by John Rosemond, *Arkansas Democrat-Gazette*, January 8, 2003, 3E.

and me. Dad's specialties were hanging the lights and helping us place long, silver icicles on the freshly cut cedar tree—one by one. My, how the years have flown by!

Decades later, as the grandkids decorated Pops' and my tree, I spotted ornaments their dad and uncle made long ago. There were pictures of little boys with big smiles, immortalized in plastic. And old Christmas cards framed with toothpicks. There were small wooden wreaths that have hung on our tree every Christmas for decades.

There's something heart-warming about holidays. The smells of freshly cut cedar and pine…the taste of homemade pumpkin pie and hot apple cider…the feel of Christmas bows…the ripping of wrapping paper…the ringing of bells and rich sounds of organs in places of worship.

Every year countless families gather in huge metropolitan areas and small country churches to celebrate Christmas.

HOLIDAYS AND BIRTHDAYS

Here are some of our family's favorite old and new holiday and birthday traditions.

Christmas:

Toothpick ornaments: First, cut some old Christmas cards into a shape similar to a small house—two walls and a pitched roof. Then glue two or three layers of toothpicks along the perimeter, making a "frame." After this dries, slip a hook or paperclip through the toothpicks, and the masterpieces are ready to be hung on the Christmas tree. Grandkids could date and sign the back of these handmade ornaments, making one more memory, for one more Christmas Day.

~

Pine straw bed for Baby Jesus: When our children were small, one of our favorite Christmas traditions was making a pine straw bed for baby Jesus (instead of pine straw, you could use pieces of hay, balls of cotton, etc.). We'd set up the Nativity with everything except the figure of Jesus. Near the Nativity we filled a small basket with straw.

Whenever family members did secret acts of kindness to honor Christ (such as making someone's bed, taking out the trash, giving an elderly neighbor cookies, and more) they would secretly place a piece of pine straw on the manger floor. Then, on Christmas Day, the figure of baby Jesus was placed on the bed that had been made as acts of worship.

~

Gingerbread houses: Our family has made countless gingerbread houses together. This tradition began when our children were very small and now it continues with the grandkids. Each grandchild decorates their own unique gingerbread house. Here's the recipe.

141

Basic Corn Syrup Gingerbread Dough[44]

9 cups unsifted flour
1 tablespoon grated orange or lemon rind
  (optional)
1 1/2 tablespoons ground cinnamon
1 tablespoon ground ginger
1/2 teaspoon salt
2 cups light corn syrup
1 1/2 cups light brown sugar firmly packed
1 1/4 cups butter

- Combine flour, orange or lemon rind, cinnamon, ginger, and salt in a large bowl.
- Stir together corn syrup, brown sugar, and butter in a 3-quart saucepan. Cook over medium heat, stirring constantly, until butter is melted and ingredients are well mixed.
- Pour liquid mixture into flour mixture and stir until blended.
- Form dough into a ball and knead until smooth and pliable.
- Roll out dough and cut into 1/4" thickness, using a lightly floured rolling pin.
- Cut out desired shapes for houses and gingerbread men.
- Use cardboard to make a pattern for the roof and sides (cut two of each shape). The following are the dimensions we use.

---

[44] Adapted from a recipe that appeared years ago in the *Arkansas Democrat-Gazette*.

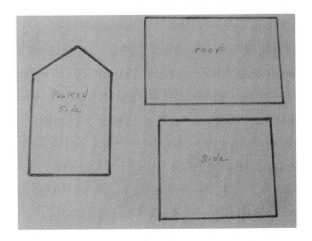

Roof—5 1/4" x 3 1/2"
Side—4 1/4" x 3 1/2"
Peaked side —2 3/4" x 3 1/2" (the point is
on top.

(The **peak of the triangle** is 4 1/2" from the
base of the rectangle it sits on.)

- You can make the houses as large or small as you
  like by changing the dimensions. Use cookie
  cutters to make gingerbread men, Christmas
  trees, stars, etc.
- Put shapes on cookie sheets that have been
  covered with parchment paper. Bake at 350
  degrees until shapes are firm and lightly
  browned —about 12 minutes.
- Completely cool shapes on racks before
  assembling.

Frosting for Gingerbread House

3 egg whites (if possible, at room
    temperature)
1-pound box powdered sugar
½ teaspoon cream of tartar

- First, beat the egg whites with the cream of tartar until stiff. Add powdered sugar and beat at medium or high speed until stiff.
- Cover with damp cloth. Makes about 2 cups of icing.
- Put the houses together with the frosting, and also use it to attach decorations and make icicles. Allow the frosting to dry on the gingerbread house at least one hour before decorating. I allow the houses to dry overnight.

Here is a picture of a gingerbread house that one of my grandchildren made:

Easter:

Do you have any Easter traditions? Perhaps an annual egg hunt with the kids or attending a sunrise service on Easter Sunday.

But have you ever made Resurrection Rolls? They are easy to make, delicious, and open up spiritual conversations.

As the grandkids and I made these Easter treats, with their hollow centers, we talked about why Jesus' tomb was empty. The simple answer? He arose! (John 20:1-18)

Resurrection Rolls
(The baked rolls will be hollow.)

> 1 can of refrigerated crescent dinner rolls (8)
> 8 large marshmallows
> 2 tablespoons ground cinnamon
> 2 tablespoons white sugar
> 1/4 cup melted butter

- Preheat oven to 400 degrees.
- Lightly grease a baking sheet.
- Mix cinnamon and sugar together.
- Separate crescent rolls into individual triangles.
- Insert a fork into a marshmallow, dip marshmallow into melted butter and roll in sugar mixture.
- Place one coated marshmallow into the center of a dough triangle.
- Carefully wrap the dough around the marshmallow. Be sure and pinch the seams together to seal in the marshmallow as it will melt when baked. (A few of the seams of my grandkids' rolls were not pinched tightly and the marshmallow melted onto the cookie sheet instead of being absorbed into the roll. So, as one who knows, double-check that the seams are pinched tightly.)
- Bake in preheated oven until golden brown, about 15 minutes.

146

Easter Bunny Cake

Rita Goodgame has made Easter Bunny Cakes for a half of a century! They are easy to make and oh, so cute! Here's Rita's recipe.

- Use a yellow cake mix and ready-made icing.
- Bake a one-layer cake, using an eight- or nine-inch cake pan.
- Cut cooled layer in half.
- Place some icing in the middle of a plate where the Bunny Cake will stand.
- For the bunny's body, ice flat sides of the two halves; stand them upright on cut edge.
- Cut ears from pink construction paper (cover tip of the bottom of ears in plastic wrap before inserting into cake).
- To form the head, cut a 1-inch wedge towards end of layer, leaving about an inch of cake on the plate for the nose, etc. Ears

will be placed in this upright space. Icing will hold ears up and will cover rest of head to hold eyes and nose.

- Place the 1-inch wedge at other end of the cake to form bunny tail; cover with icing.
- Can use jelly beans or gumdrops for the eyes and nose.[45]

Children do not always like coconut. So, instead of coating the bunny with coconut you may want to color the coconut with green food coloring and use it for the grass.

Resurrection Eggs

FamilyLife (www.familylife.com) sells a wonderful product called Resurrection Eggs®, a dozen plastic eggs that contain small objects representing Christ's crucifixion. The twelfth egg is actually empty, representing Jesus' empty tomb. Pops and I have given these to our younger grandchildren for many years, whether they lived near us or far away.

Thanksgiving:

A favorite tradition for our family is a Thanksgiving tree. We use a small plastic gumdrop tree. But

---

[45] Picture and recipe by Rita Goodgame. Used with permission.

instead of attaching gumdrops to its branches, our tree is covered with small notes of thanks to God for what He has done during the year.

During the weeks leading up to Thanksgiving, Jim and I, the kids, and grandkids periodically jot down things we're thankful for. We do this on colorful leaves made from construction paper. We ask long-distance kids and grandkids to email or text us what they want written on their leaves.

Then we hole-punch the paper leaves and attach them to the tree. On Thanksgiving Day, we place the tree in the center of our dining room table. After we eat the annual feast, we take turns reading what is written on each leaf, guessing who wrote it. Whoever guesses the correct person gets to choose the next leaf.

I save the colorful leaves in envelopes (dated by year). At first, the grandkids thanked God for "family, my teacher, Jesus, my turtle...donuts." But as they have gotten older, the list has changed.

Last year the gratitude leaves included "my wonderful family that loves me, Jesus dying for us, the outdoors, laughter, taste buds, this food we are eating, Memaw and Pepaw, Nana and Pops...my friends."

Birthdays:

Does your family have special birthday traditions??

Birthdays were big deals in my family—complete with fancy cakes, family, and parties. But for my husband, birthdays were not that big of a deal. He actually prefers a birthday pie to a cake.

Over the years our traditions have blended together into something that fits our family. But two favorite traditions are the birthday letters (mentioned in chapter 3) and a special gift when a grandchild becomes a teenager.

Perhaps long after Pops and I are gone, our grandchildren will pull out the old birthday letters we sent them. As they read the then tattered letters, I hope they will sense Pops' and my love for them, our faith in Christ, and our belief in eternity.

My friend Joanie Stineman also sends birthday letters, but she chooses a theme for each year. For example, Joanie knows her granddaughter's friends mean a lot to her. So when her granddaughter, Ella, turned fourteen, Joanie sent her a picture of two elephants standing side by side with their trunks wrapped around each other. She wrote, "50 years ago, I was a 14-year-old girl." Then Joanie told Ella a story from her own teenage years.

And when one of her grandsons turned ten, her letter included what was going on in the boy's great-grandfathers' lives when they were his age.

When our grandkids turn thirteen, Jim and I give them a photo book filled with pictures of their life—from infancy to thirteen. We've made three of these so far, and have five more to go.

PUTTING IT INTO ACTION

1. What are some traditions that were special to you as a child?

- Christmas—

- Easter—

- Thanksgiving—

- Birthday—

2. When will you talk to your grandchild about one of your favorite traditions?

3. Who began certain traditions in your family? If you do not know, how could you find out?

4. What are your grandchild's favorite holiday and birthday traditions?

5. If you do not know your grandchild's favorite holiday and birthday traditions, plan some one-on-one time to have this conversation. Write below when you will do this.

6. What family traditions are important to your mother or dad, to your son-in-law or daughter-in-law? Consider including at least one of them in your annual celebrations.

7. Begin writing your grandchild an annual birthday letter. Decide if you want to include family pictures, stories, etc. Write some of your ideas below.

8. Review the ideas presented in this chapter. Choose one or two you would like to begin. Write them below and also in *My Grandparenting Connection.*

Chapter 14

Your Legacy

One name that is special to me is MeMe. It's special because a very special little girl calls me by that name—my granddaughter! And before that her mother called my mother by that name. So it has become a link from the present to the past and to the future.

—LaRue Launius

Back in 1983, a photograph of a white-haired woman standing in front of a deteriorating wooden home graced the cover of *Rural Arkansas* magazine. More than just a dwelling, the structure had sheltered many generations. Its creaking wood had witnessed the joys and laughter of young children and the heartache of deep loss.

The caption said the old homeplace now sighs and sometimes "groans with its memories and its years…It is a reflection of a small bit of heaven. It is home."[46]

Much like this once beloved home, grandparents have witnessed much. Their aging hands have held the soft skin of new life. And they've also brushed

---

[46] *Arkansas Living Magazine*, March 2012, 39.

away far too many tears from sorrow and regret. Yet most grandparents long for their grandchildren to feel the warmth and security of their love.

Some, like Sharon Ball's grandmother, leave behind a bit of heaven. In 2010, Sharon wrote about her grandmother's life.

Saying Goodbye

This has been a difficult week for my family as we have said goodbye to my grandmother who we all will miss. The homegoing celebration was yesterday, July 14, 2010, and my grandmother was 83 years old. During the memorial service, as friends and family talked about how she touched their lives, I was amazed at all of the new things I learned about her.

For example, I never knew until yesterday that my grandmother graduated from Florida A&M University with a degree in Home Economics in 1951. I had always known that she was very active in her church and community, but I didn't know the extent of her far-reaching involvement until yesterday.

As a powerful woman of God, my grandmother lived her life in a way that truly reflected God's love and provided a living example of how to be in the world, but not of the world. She was the kind of person who never, and I mean never, gossiped about other folks in any way, shape, or form, and she was not a hypocrite.

She had faith, but she also had works that went along with her faith, and she helped all of God's children to the best of her ability. She was an amazing mother and grandmother, full of wisdom, guidance, love and patience that touched and changed lives. I know she is with Jesus, and I can't wait to see her again when our Lord returns.

I'll leave you with these few words…love your family and show your love while there is still life left in your body. …[47]

Memories

What do you remember about your grandparents? What do you hope your grandchildren will remember about you?

Will they know what was important to you, where you graduated from high school or college, and how you helped in your community? Will they have more than a quick glimpse of your faith?

One of my favorite memories of my mother happened by accident. We were watching a video of a long-ago family reunion, and there was my mom, wearing a bright yellow sweater, enjoying a meal with the family. As I watched the video clip, it soon became obvious that it was taken by mistake. I had been trying to take a picture of my son Chris and his family when I hit the video button in error.

Now years later, as I replayed the mistaken videotape, I heard my voice. "Squeeze together," I said, as a grandchild finished a bite of food and gave a big smile. Next, with almost panic, I said something like, "I think this thing is videotaping. What should I do?"

The lens went up to the ceiling and way down to the floor. It seemed to go in circles. The camera was out of control, or more accurately, I was out of control.

---

[47]"A Break from the Norm." © 2010 Sharon Ball. Used with permission.

155

"I don't know what to do," I repeated, as my son tried to tell me how to turn the video off, "Hit the button...the button!"

Success! The videotaping stopped and the screen went dark. I must have proceeded to take some pictures, thinking I was recovering from a mistake.

But as I watched that long-ago video of my mom eating a meal with the family, saw her bright smile and kind eyes, I so wished the filming would have run much longer. That I could have seen another frame or two, or twenty, or two hundred of my sweet mother.

I wished that I could have somehow jumped into that videotape to give my mom one more hug, one last kiss. But that is no longer possible.

Yes, tomorrow is not promised. May we make the most of today.

Mark Batterson's grandfather made a big impact on his life. Elmer Johnson died when Mark was only six years old. "My Grandpa Johnson had a habit of kneeling by his bed at night, taking off his hearing aid, and praying for his family," Mark said. "He couldn't hear himself, but everyone else in the house could. Few things are more powerful than hearing someone who intercedes on your behalf. His voiceprint left an imprint on my soul."[48]

And my daughter-in-law's beloved Mamaw will never be forgotten by her or our grandkids. Many

---

[48] *Praying Circles Around the Lives of Your Children* by Mark Batterson. © 2014 by Mark Batterson. Published by Zondervan, 10.

years ago, Tonya wrote this touching poem about her grandmother:

A Special Lady
by Tonya Larmoyeux

There's a lady I've known all my life
who has been my inspiration.
She's not fancy or dressed in jewels,
yet she holds my fascination.

She unselfishly took care of nine children
from birth 'til their adult years—
Not a mere thanks did she ever expect
for her dedication, turmoil, and tears.

She's stubborn and independent
Two of her most admiring traits.
Her godliness and her loving heart
are only two of her virtues that make her great.

She doesn't think she has much to offer
because she is physically unable
but she's given me more than anyone has
because I've learned from her example.

I hope that she doesn't leave this world
without knowing how I feel.
She is loved by all who know her.
My, how God has used her well.[49]

---

[49] Used with permission.

An Unexpected Surprise

Yes, Tonya's grandmother made a big impact on her life, as did my grandmother, Nana.

As I was writing this book, an unexpected thing happened. I ran across an old email from a distant relative who had a picture of Nana, my grandmother, Grandpa's wife.

I contacted her and a whole new world was opened to me. I discovered names and pictures of ancestors I never knew. Now some of my distant memories as a child are coming into focus as I continue to piece together my own story and legacy.

Because of the caring efforts of one woman to preserve our family history, the "dry bones" of my ancestors are speaking to me today, and I will pass on their legacy.

For me, my grandparenting journey is far from over. There are so many connections with my grandchildren that I want to make...perhaps thousands of photographs that need to be identified... lots of stories to be written...countless prayers to be said.

Come with me on your own one-of-a-kind grand-parenting journey. If you haven't started already, let's begin.

PUTTING IT INTO ACTION

1. What are a few of your favorite memories of your grandmothers or grandfathers? (continue on next page).

158

(continued from page 158)

2. What is the most important lesson a grandparent taught you? How did they teach you this?

3. What do you hope your great-great-great grandchildren will know about you one day? Answer below and also in *My Grandparenting Connection.*

Appendix

- *My Grandparenting Connection*
  (Where you design your unique
  one-of-a-kind grandparent connection)

- 10 Ways to Remember the Day a
  Grandchild Is Born

- Christmas Do's and Don'ts for
  Mothers- and Daughters-in-Law

My Grandparenting Connection

*Where you design your unique
one-of-a-kind grandparent connection*

Your answers to the following questions will help you form unique ways to connect with your one-of-a-kind grandchild. After you have read this book, periodically review and update this section.

Chapter 1: Begin Your Grandparenting Connection

1. The three chapters that interest me the most are:

2. I hope my grandchildren will remember this about me:

Chapter 2: Nearby Grandparenting

1. Two or three ideas from this chapter that I would like to use are:

Chapter 3: Long-Distance Grandparenting

1. Two or three ideas from this chapter that I would like to use are:

Chapter 4: Your Prayers

1. A prayer idea given in this chapter that I want to begin is:

Chapter 5: Your Personal Stories

1. The working title of my first story is:

I would like to finish writing it by the following date:

2. This is where I will keep my stories:

3. My second story will be about this memory:

I would like to finish writing this story by the following date:

Chapter 6: Your Faith Stories

1. Here are a few sentences about a significant time when faith caused me to take a defining path in my life:

I will write in detail about this by the following date:

Chapter 7: Your Ancestors

1. I would like my grandchild _____ _____(name) to personally interview me about my life. We will do this on _____(date).

2. My grandchild and I will begin to research our family by exploring the following topic together:

Chapter 8: Your Treasured Possessions

1. I will discuss with _____(name) by _____(date) what family possessions they would like to have one day.

Chapter 9: Your Family Photographs

1. The photo idea from this chapter that I want to begin first is:

Chapter 10: Your Life Lessons

1. I will discuss the following historical event with my grandchild (an event I personally experienced):

2. I will discuss the following turning points in my life with my grandchild (one from my successes and one from my failures, struggles, and regrets) by _____ (date).

- From successes:

- From failures, struggles, and regrets:

Chapter 11: Your Unconditional Love

1. To help my grandchild better sense my unconditional love, I will:

Chapter 12: Your Family Recipes

1. One of my favorite family recipes is:

I chose this recipe because:

2. One or two recipe ideas from this chapter that I would like to use are:

Chapter 13: Your Holiday and Birthday Traditions

1. One or two ideas from this chapter that I would like to begin are:

Chater 14: Your Legacy

1. I hope my great-great-great grandchildren will know this about me:

10 Ways to Remember the Day a Grandchild Is Born[50]

Our then six-year-old grandson and his eight-year-old sister were staying with Jim and me when their little sister was born. I asked them to write what they thought about the new baby.

Big brother printed that she was "so cyout [cute]"… and that she looks like a "cimunk [chipmunk]." Big sis, on the other hand wrote in cursive, "… For the first time in my life I saw my baby sister, and she saw me. I held her and she stopped crying …"

I also did two things to remember that day: took a picture of the morning fog and bought a newspaper. (Maybe she'll want to know about the weather and what was going on in the world when she took her first breath.)

Here are ten ways to remember the day a grandchild was born:

1. Write the thoughts and feelings you had when you first held your grandchild; describe what happened on the day he was born.

---

[50] Adapted from "10 Ways to Remember the Day a Child is Born" by Mary May Larmoyeux, https://legacyconnection.org/10-ways-remember-day-child-born. Accessed on 4/19/2019.

2. Jot down the child's full name and date of birth in your Bible, along with a favorite Scripture that you will pray for her life.

3. If possible, buy a newspaper or magazine on the day your grandchild is born. You can show it to him one day. Or print the homepage of an online newspaper.

4. Save the baby's first booties, and frame them with some pictures from her "birth-day."

5. If you live away from loved ones, take advantage of today's technology—use Skype or FaceTime to connect.

6. Plant a tree in your yard, and take a picture when you do this. (Someday you can show this to your grandchild).

7. If your grandchild has siblings, video the first time they meet their new brother or sister, and ask them what they think about the new addition.

8. Ask grandparents and great-grandparents to write the baby a "birth-day" letter, including their dreams for the child.

9. Take a picture of the hospital or home where the baby was born. Jot down the name of the doctor or mid-wife who delivered him.

10. On your grandchild's first birthday, write her a letter recalling the first day of her life. Put this in her baby book.

Christmas Do's and Don'ts for Mothers- and Daughters-in-Law

I asked friends and family how mothers- and daughters-in law could deepen their relationships during the often too hectic Christmas season. How can their mutual celebrations be marked with peace and grace?

My friend Cindy said during the holidays, she and her daughter-in-law like "to sit and talk and share and connect in person."

And Liz says it's important to go into holiday times with family by having a heart of service. Thinking, "What can I do for you?" and not, "What you can you do for me?"

Here are some helpful holiday do's and don'ts for mothers- and daughters-in-law. Carefully consider the "don'ts." And then choose some of the do's that meet the unique needs of your family.

Don't:

...ignore who Christmas is about.
...give unsolicited advice.

...personalize choices that differ from your desires.

...demean your mother- or daughter-in-law, especially in front of the grandkids.

...assume a role that is not yours to have. For example, don't take authority that belongs to parents.

...have a "someone owes me" attitude.

...enter the holidays presuming what you want for a family Christmas gathering is what everyone else in the family wants.

...intrude on your in-laws' plans—whether a daughter- or mother-in-law.

...clean your mother- or daughter-in-law's kitchen or home without her permission.

Do:

...Focus on your relationship with the Babe of Christmas.

...let go of expectations.

...leave room for spontaneity.

...have a cookie exchange with mothers, daughters, mothers-in-law, and daughters-in-law. Include a long-distance mother- or daughter-in-law in the fun via Facebook or Skype.

...ask what your mother- or daughter-in-law wants for a Christmas gift.

...simplify gift-giving for all by drawing names for holiday gifts.

...begin some new family traditions with your daughter- or mother-in-law such as spending a day together Christmas shopping.

...take time to share a cup of hot coffee or tea and

talk about holiday expectations. (Mail special teas or coffees to out of town in-laws.)

...ask, "How can I help?"

...include a multi-generational family photo in your holiday plans. Give advance notice of when and where it will be taken.

...participate in a service project together.

...share encouraging Bible verses via email or text during December. Choose ones that bring you God's peace and remind you of the true meaning of the season.

...ask your mother- or daughter-in-law, "What Christmas traditions matter to you?"

...share a favorite holiday recipe with each other.

...talk or text about Christmas celebrations you enjoyed as children.

...lend a hand with Christmas meal preparations.

...communicate and encourage honesty in what people want to do.

...if your mother- or daughter-in-law has a favorite beverage (i.e., Peppermint tea, Dr. Pepper, coffee with real cream, etc.) be sure and offer it to her when you get together.

...on the day of your Christmas family celebration, bring out a past gift that was given by an in-law. You may also want to pull out a treasured toy from the attic that was once a favorite of a now adult child.

...include a few simple recipes for the family holiday meal. Doing this will make it easy for others to help with meal preparations.

...for out-of-town in-laws, put a welcome sign in front of your house.

...arrange for a special area where kids can play, color, do crafts, and more to help in-laws truly visit.

...save some small tasks for someone who asks how they can help.

...look at photo albums together during the family Christmas gathering.

...make time to tell family stories. How did your daughter-in-law celebrate Christmas as a child? What did your mother-in-law do to make Christmas special for her son?

...generously give grace (undeserved kindness) to one another.

Thank you for reading this book!

You can visit Mary May Larmoyeux at
www.legacyconnection.org.

Made in the USA
Columbia, SC
04 August 2020

14690537R00107